Nestlé®

TOLL HOUSE®

RECIPE COLLECTION

BEEKMAN HOUSE
New York

CONTENTS

THE TOLL HOUSE KITCHENS
SUCCESS GUIDE TO BAKING **3**

COOKIES **5**

PIES **28**

CAKES & FROSTINGS **37**

BREADS **56**

CANDY **70**

DESSERTS **78**

INDEX **94**

Copyright © Nestlé Foods Corporation, 1987.
All rights reserved.

NESTLÉ TOLL HOUSE, CHOCO-BAKE,
TASTER'S CHOICE and NESCAFÉ are registered
trademarks of Nestlé Foods Corporation.

NESCAFÉ CLASSIC, LITTLE BITS and TOLL
HOUSE KITCHENS are trademarks of Nestlé
Foods Corporation.

Library of Congress Catalog Card Number:
87-61999

Manufactured in the United States of America
h g f e d c b a

ISBN: 0-517-62294-7

This edition published by:
Beekman House
Distributed by Crown Publishers, Inc., 225 Park
Avenue South, New York, New York 10003.

Pictured on the front cover: Double Chocolate
Cookies and Chocolate Orange Granola Cookies
(*see page* 19).

Pictured on the back cover (*clockwise from top left*):
Chocolate Filled Cream Puff Ring (*see page* 80);
Frozen Strawberry Fudge Pie (*see page* 34); Toll
House™ Crumbcake (*see page* 63); Chocolate Mint
Layer Cake (*see page* 41).

THE TOLL HOUSE KITCHENS
SUCCESS GUIDE TO BAKING

Welcome to the exciting world of baking and snack-making with Nestlé Toll House Morsels! For over 50 years, Nestlé has led the way in producing the very highest quality baking ingredients, beginning with our famous Nestlé Toll House semi-sweet chocolate morsels . . . to the entire tempting array of Toll House products. We've come a long, delicious way since the introduction of the Original Toll House Cookie. Today, our recipes range from quick and easy snacks to indulgently rich and elegant desserts. Whether treasured Toll House favorites or brand new ideas, all of our recipes are developed and tested by the Toll House Kitchens . . . the experts on chocolate and desserts.

Baking Techniques

Separating Eggs: Tap the side of the egg on the edge of a bowl or cup to crack the shell. Pass the yolk from shell to shell, dropping the white into a cup before adding it to the other whites in the bowl. If a little yolk gets into the whites, scoop it out with part of the shell. The presence of any yolk in the whites can ruin them.

Beating Egg Whites: Egg whites may be beaten with an electric mixer, rotary eggbeater or balloon style whisk. Bowl and beater must be clean and dry because even a small amount of grease or oil can prevent the whites from whipping properly. Beat the whites slowly, gradually increasing the speed as they begin to foam. Beat only until they hold shape or point. Caution: do not beat egg whites ahead of time. They should be folded in *immediately* after they are beaten.

Whipping Cream: Cream may be whipped with electric mixer, rotary eggbeater or balloon style whisk. Cream, bowl and beaters should be very cold for best results. To avoid spattering, beat slowly, gradually increasing speed as cream thickens. It's best not to whip cream too far ahead of time or it will separate slightly. If this happens, mix briefly with a wire whisk.

Folding Ingredients: Many recipes call for folding beaten egg whites or whipped cream into another mixture. Both egg whites and whipped cream contain air in the form of many small bubbles. Folding, rather than mixing, is done to retain the air in the mixture. Start with a large bowl containing the heavier mixture. Place a portion of the egg whites or whipped cream on top of the heavier mixture. Using a circular motion with a rubber spatula, cut down through center of mixture across bottom of bowl, lifting up and over. After each fold, rotate the bowl slightly in order to incorporate the ingredients as evenly as possible. Fold in remaining egg whites or whipped cream until uniformly but lightly combined.

Measuring Dry Ingredients: Use the standard graded sets of four: ¼ cup, ⅓ cup, ½ cup and 1 cup. Spoon dry ingredients into measure and level off with a metal spatula.

Measuring Liquid Ingredients: Use a glass or plastic measuring cup with a pour spout. With the cup sitting on a flat surface, read at eye level. Fill to exactly the line indicated.

Words To Bake By

Beat: To thoroughly combine ingredients and incorporate air with a rapid, regular motion. This may be done with a wire whisk, rotary eggbeater or electric mixer.

Blend: To thoroughly combine two or more ingredients.

Chill: To refrigerate until cold.

Cream: To combine two or more ingredients by beating until the mixture is light and well blended.

Cut In: To combine solid fat with dry ingredients by using a pastry blender or two knives in a scissor motion until particles are of the desired size.

Drizzle: To sprinkle drops of glaze or icing over food in random manner from tines of a fork or the end of a spoon.

Full Rolling Boil: To cook a mixture until it appears to rise in the pan. The surface billows rather than just bubbles.

Glaze: To coat with a liquid, a thin icing or a jelly either before or after food is cooked.

Mixing Just Until Moistened: Combining dry ingredients with liquid ingredients until dry ingredients are thoroughly moistened but mixture is still lumpy.

Packed Brown Sugar: Brown sugar pressed into measuring cup with a spoon. Sugar will hold its shape when cup is inverted.

Simmer: To cook in liquid just below the boiling point. Bubbles form slowly just below the surface.

Soft Peaks: Egg whites or cream beaten to the stage where mixture forms soft rounded peaks when beaters are removed.

Stiff Peaks: Egg whites or cream beaten to the stage where mixture holds stiff pointed peaks when beaters are removed.

Chocolate: Its Care & Handling

It's no surprise that chocolate is America's favorite flavor. However, as a natural product made principally from cocoa beans, chocolate does have certain characteristics that affect the way it should be stored and used for best results.

Storing Chocolate
The key words are *cool, dry* and *low* humidity! Storage temperature should be between 60° and 78°F., with relative humidity at less than 50%. It's all right to refrigerate chocolate, but wrap it tightly so it won't absorb odors. Airtight

wrapping will also prevent moisture from condensing on the chocolate when it is removed from the refrigerator. Chocolate becomes hard and brittle when cold, so allow it to come to room temperature before using.

A Tip About Milk Chocolate Morsels

Don't use milk chocolate morsels in baked desserts that do not call for melting the morsels before blending them in. The milk content causes them to become hard when they are baked. You may substitute milk chocolate morsels for semi-sweet morsels in recipes such as frostings or sauces that call for melting the morsels.

There's No Love In "Bloom," But No Harm Either

Chocolate has a high content of cocoa butter. When stored at temperatures that fluctuate from hot to cold, chocolate can develop "bloom"—a gray film caused by the cocoa butter rising to the surface. This dulls the rich brown chocolate color but does not affect the flavor. When the chocolate melts, it regains its attractive color. Don't hesitate to use it.

MELTING CHOCOLATE PERFECTLY

Important Reminder: Even the smallest drop of moisture from a wet spoon or steam from a double boiler can cause melted chocolate to become lumpy. If this occurs, all is not lost. Stir in 1 tablespoon vegetable shortening (not butter) for every 3 ounces of chocolate. Butter is not used because it contains water. Stir continuously until the consistency is smooth and even.

Top of Stove Method: All varieties of Nestlé Toll House Morsels can be melted using this traditional method. Place the amount of morsels you want to melt in the top of a clean, dry double boiler. Place over hot (not boiling) water, stirring occasionally until smooth. Note: water in bottom pan should be 1 inch below top pan for best results.

Microwave Method: All varieties of morsels can also be melted using a microwave oven. Simply place the amount of morsels you want to melt in a dry glass measuring cup twice the size (i.e., to melt 1 cup of morsels use a 2-cup measuring cup). Microwave on *high* for 1 minute; stir. Microwave on *high* for 30 seconds longer; stir. It is necessary to stir the morsels thoroughly to determine if they are completely melted because they retain their original shape even in the melted state. Because microwave ovens may differ in power levels, consult your "User's Guide" for specific directions for your particular model.

RECIPE CALLS FOR:	YOU MAY USE:
1 ounce (1 square) unsweetened baking chocolate	3 ounces (½ cup) Nestlé Toll House semi-sweet chocolate morsels. Decrease shortening 1 tablespoon and sugar ¼ cup.
3 ounces (3 squares) semi-sweet baking chocolate	3 ounces (½ cup) Nestlé Toll House semi-sweet chocolate morsels.
¼ cup unsweetened cocoa powder	3 ounces (½ cup) Nestlé Toll House semi-sweet chocolate morsels. Decrease shortening 1 tablespoon and sugar ¼ cup.

Baking Pan Options

If a recipe calls for a size of baking pan you don't have, chances are you can use what you *do* have on hand. Use the following list for practical substitutions. But remember, changing pan sizes will alter baking time. Smaller pans of the same shape will take *less* baking time. Shallow pans will take less time than loaf pans with higher sides. *Tip:* Keep a record of pan size changes and baking times for future use.

RECIPE CALLS FOR:	YOU MAY USE:
9×5×3-inch loaf pan	two 7½×3¾×2¼-inch loaf pans OR three 5½×3¼×2¼-inch loaf pans.
8½×4½×2½-inch loaf pan	two 5½×3¼×2¼-inch loaf pans OR one 1-pound coffee can.
10-inch fluted tube pan	one 10×4-inch tube pan OR one 12-cup ring mold OR two 9×5×3-inch loaf pans.
13×9×2-inch pan	two 9-inch round pans OR two 8-inch round pans OR two 8-inch square pans.
One 9-inch round pan	one 8-inch square pan.
Two 9-inch round pans	three 8-inch round pans.

Substitution Magic

How many times has it happened to you? You're missing one item the recipe calls for and you're stuck. Don't despair; just try one of these easy sleight-of-hand substitutes.

RECIPE CALLS FOR:	YOU MAY USE:
1 teaspoon **baking powder**	¼ teaspoon baking soda + ½ teaspoon cream of tartar.
½ cup firmly packed **brown sugar**	½ cup sugar mixed with 2 tablespoons molasses.
1 cup **buttermilk**	1 tablespoon lemon juice or vinegar and milk to make 1 cup.
½ cup **corn syrup**	½ cup sugar + 2 tablespoons liquid.
1 tablespoon **cornstarch**	2 tablespoons flour OR 4 teaspoons quick-cooking tapioca.
1 cup **light cream**	⅞ cup milk + 3 tablespoons butter.
1 cup **whole milk**	1 cup skim milk + 2 teaspoons butter OR ½ cup evaporated milk + ½ cup water.
1 teaspoon grated **orange** or **lemon rind**	½ teaspoon dried peel.

COOKIES

Butterscotch Apricot Streusel Bars

Makes 3 dozen 2×1½-inch bars

FILLING:
One 8-ounce package dried apricots
1½ cups water

COOKIE LAYER:
  2 cups whole wheat flour, divided
1⅔ cups quick oats, uncooked
  ¾ teaspoon salt
  ½ teaspoon baking soda
  ¾ cup molasses
  ½ cup butter, softened
  ½ of 12-ounce package (1 cup) Nestlé Toll House
    butterscotch flavored morsels

Filling: In medium saucepan, combine apricots and water. Cook over medium heat, stirring occasionally, until water evaporates and mixture is thickened. Set aside.

Cookie Layer: Preheat oven to 375°F. In small bowl, combine 1¾ cups flour, oats, salt and baking soda; set aside. In large bowl, combine molasses and butter; beat until creamy. Gradually beat in flour mixture. Remove 1 cup of mixture and place in small bowl; set aside. Press remaining mixture into foil-lined 13×9-inch baking pan. Top with Filling; set aside. Add remaining ¼ cup flour to reserved mixture; stir until crumbs form. Stir in Nestlé Toll House butterscotch flavored morsels. Sprinkle crumb mixture on top. Bake at 375°F. for 20–25 minutes. Cool completely on wire rack. Cut into 2×1½-inch bars.

Milk Chocolate Pecan Bars

Makes 4½ dozen 2×1-inch bars

COOKIE BASE:
  1 cup all-purpose flour
  ½ cup firmly packed brown sugar
  ½ teaspoon baking soda
  ¼ cup butter

TOPPING:
One 11½-ounce package (2 cups) Nestlé Toll House
    milk chocolate morsels
  2 eggs
  ¼ cup firmly packed brown sugar
  1 teaspoon vanilla extract
  ¼ teaspoon salt
  1 cup chopped pecans, divided

Cookie Base: Preheat oven to 350°F. In large bowl, combine flour, brown sugar and baking soda; mix well. With pastry blender or 2 knives, cut in butter until mixture resembles fine crumbs. Press evenly into greased 13×9-inch baking pan. Bake at 350°F. for 10 minutes.

Topping: Melt over hot (not boiling) water, Nestlé Toll House milk chocolate morsels; stir until smooth. Remove from heat. In medium bowl, combine eggs, brown sugar, vanilla extract and salt; beat 2 minutes at high speed. Add melted morsels; mix well. Stir in ½ cup pecans.

Pour Topping over Cookie Base; sprinkle with remaining ½ cup pecans. Bake at 350°F. for 20 minutes. Cool completely on wire rack; cut into 2×1-inch bars.

Butterscotch Date Surprise

Butterscotch Date Surprise

Makes 5 dozen 1½-inch cookies

COOKIE:
1¼ cups all-purpose flour
1¼ cups whole wheat flour
¼ teaspoon baking soda
¼ teaspoon salt
½ cup butter, softened
½ cup firmly packed brown sugar
¼ cup sugar
2 eggs
1 teaspoon vanilla extract

FILLING:
One 8-ounce package pitted dates
1 cup chopped walnuts
½ cup water
¼ cup sugar
1 teaspoon grated lemon rind
½ of 12-ounce package (1 cup) Nestlé Toll House butterscotch flavored morsels

Cookie: In medium bowl, combine flours, baking soda and salt; set aside. In large bowl, combine butter, brown sugar and sugar; beat until creamy. Beat in eggs and vanilla extract. Gradually add flour mixture. Divide dough in half. Wrap each half in plastic wrap; chill thoroughly.

Filling: In blender container or food processor, combine dates and walnuts. Process at high speed until pureed. In medium saucepan, combine date mixture, water, sugar and lemon rind. Cook over medium heat, stirring constantly, until mixture thickens. Chill. Stir in Nestlé Toll House butterscotch flavored morsels. *(continued)*

Preheat oven to 375°F. On lightly floured board, roll ½ of dough into 15×9-inch rectangle. Cut crosswise into five 3-inch strips. Spread ¼ cup Filling down center of each strip. Fold sides up and seal. Repeat with remaining dough and Filling. Place on ungreased cookie sheet, seam side down. Bake at 375°F. for 15–17 minutes. Cool 10 minutes. Remove from cookie sheet; cool completely on wire rack. Cut into 1½-inch cookies.

Original Toll House® Cookies

Makes 5 dozen 2¼-inch cookies

2¼ cups all-purpose flour
1 teaspoon baking soda
1 teaspoon salt
1 cup butter, softened
¾ cup sugar
¾ cup firmly packed brown sugar
1 teaspoon vanilla extract
2 eggs
One 12-ounce package (2 cups) Nestlé Toll House semi-sweet chocolate morsels
1 cup chopped nuts

Preheat oven to 375°F. In small bowl, combine flour, baking soda and salt; set aside. In large bowl, combine butter, sugar, brown sugar and vanilla extract; beat until creamy. Beat in eggs. Gradually add flour mixture. Stir in Nestlé Toll House semi-sweet chocolate morsels and nuts. Drop by level tablespoonfuls onto ungreased cookie sheets. Bake at 375°F. for 9–11 minutes.

Refrigerator Toll House Cookies: Prepare dough as directed. Divide dough in half; wrap both halves separately in waxed paper. Chill 1 hour or until firm. On waxed paper, shape each dough half into 15-inch log. Roll up in waxed paper; refrigerate for 30 minutes.* Preheat oven to 375°F. Cut each log into thirty ½-inch slices. Place on ungreased cookie sheets. Bake at 375°F. for 8–10 minutes. Makes 5 dozen 2¼-inch cookies.

Pan Cookie: Spread dough into greased 15½×10½×1-inch baking pan. Bake at 375°F. for 20–25 minutes. Cool completely. Cut into thirty-five 2-inch squares.

*May be stored up to 1 week in refrigerator or freeze up to 8 weeks.

Cheese Crunchers

Makes about 6 dozen 2×1-inch bars

One 12-ounce package (2 cups) Nestlé Toll House butterscotch flavored morsels
6 tablespoons butter
2 cups graham cracker crumbs
2 cups chopped walnuts
Two 8-ounce packages cream cheese, softened
½ cup sugar
4 eggs
¼ cup all-purpose flour
2 tablespoons lemon juice   *(continued)*

Preheat oven to 350°F. Combine over hot (not boiling) water, Nestlé Toll House butterscotch flavored morsels and butter; stir until morsels are melted and mixture is smooth. Transfer to large bowl; stir in graham cracker crumbs and walnuts with a fork until mixture resembles fine crumbs. Reserve 2 cups crumb mixture for topping. Press remaining mixture into ungreased 15½×10½×1-inch baking pan. Bake at 350°F. for 12 minutes.

In large bowl, combine cream cheese and sugar; beat until creamy. Add eggs, 1 at a time, beating well after each addition. Blend in flour and lemon juice. Pour evenly over hot baked crust. Sprinkle reserved crumb mixture on top. Bake at 350°F. for 25 minutes. Cool completely on wire rack; cut into 2×1-inch bars. Chill before serving.

Cheese Crunchers

Chocolate Raspberry Linzer Cookies

Chocolate Raspberry Linzer Cookies

Makes about 3 dozen 2½-inch cookies

2⅓ cups all-purpose flour
1 teaspoon baking powder
½ teaspoon cinnamon
½ teaspoon salt
1 cup sugar
¾ cup butter, softened
2 eggs
½ teaspoon almond extract
One 12-ounce package (2 cups) Nestlé Toll House semi-sweet chocolate morsels
¾ cup raspberry jam or preserves
Confectioners' sugar

(continued)

In medium bowl, combine flour, baking powder, cinnamon and salt; set aside. In large bowl, combine sugar and butter; beat until creamy. Beat in eggs and almond extract. Gradually beat in flour mixture. Divide dough in half. Wrap each half in plastic wrap; chill until firm. Preheat oven to 350°F. On lightly floured board, roll ½ of dough to ⅛-inch thickness. Cut with 2½-inch round cookie cutter. Repeat with remaining dough. Cut out 1½-inch centers from ½ of 2½-inch unbaked cookies. Reroll remaining dough and cut out cookies. Place on ungreased cookie sheets. Bake at 350°F. for 8–10 minutes. Cool completely on wire racks.

Melt over hot (not boiling) water, Nestlé Toll House semi-sweet chocolate morsels; stir until smooth. Spread 1 teaspoon chocolate on flat side of each whole cookie. Top with 1 teaspoon raspberry jam. Sprinkle confectioners' sugar on each cookie with center hole. Place on top of chocolate/jam cookies to form sandwich.

Black & White Cheesecake Brownies

Makes sixteen 2¼-inch brownies

BROWNIE BASE:

One 12-ounce package (2 cups) Nestlé Toll House
    Little Bits semi-sweet chocolate, divided
  ½ cup sugar
  ¼ cup butter, softened
  2 eggs
  1 teaspoon vanilla extract
  ½ teaspoon salt
  ⅔ cup all-purpose flour

CHEESECAKE TOPPING:

One 8-ounce package cream cheese, softened
  ½ cup sugar
  2 tablespoons butter, softened
  2 eggs
  2 tablespoons milk
  1 tablespoon all-purpose flour
  ½ teaspoon almond extract
  ¾ cup Nestlé Toll House Little Bits semi-sweet
    chocolate, reserved from 12-ounce package

Brownie Base: Preheat oven to 350°F. Melt over hot (not boiling) water, 1¼ cups Nestlé Toll House Little Bits semi-sweet chocolate; stir until smooth. Set aside. In large bowl, combine sugar and butter; beat until creamy. Add eggs, vanilla extract and salt; mix well. Add melted morsels and flour; mix well. Spread into foil-lined 9-inch square baking pan.

Cheesecake Topping: In large bowl, combine cream cheese, sugar and butter; beat until creamy. Add eggs, milk, flour and almond extract; beat well. Stir in remaining ¾ cup Nestlé Toll House Little Bits semi-sweet chocolate. Pour over Brownie Base. Bake at 350°F. for 40–45 minutes. Cool completely on wire rack; cut into 2¼-inch squares.

Chocolate Mint Pinwheels

Makes about 3½ dozen cookies

One 10-ounce package (1½ cups) Nestlé Toll House
    mint-chocolate morsels, divided
  ¾ cup butter, softened
  ⅓ cup sugar
  1 egg
  1 teaspoon vanilla extract
  2¼ cups all-purpose flour
  ½ teaspoon salt

(continued)

Melt over hot (not boiling) water, ½ cup Nestlé Toll House mint-chocolate morsels; stir until smooth. Cool to room temperature; set aside. In large bowl, combine butter and sugar; beat until creamy. Add egg and vanilla extract; beat well. Gradually beat in flour and salt. Place 1 cup of dough in small bowl. Add melted morsels; blend thoroughly. Shape into ball; flatten.* Cover with plastic wrap. Shape remaining dough into ball; flatten. Cover with plastic wrap. Chill until firm (about 1½ hours). Preheat oven to 375°F. Between sheets of waxed paper, roll each ball of dough into 13×9-inch rectangle. Remove top layers of waxed paper. Invert chocolate dough onto plain dough. Peel off waxed paper. Starting from the long side, roll up jelly roll style. Cut into ¼-inch slices; place on ungreased cookie sheet. Bake at 375°F. for 7–8 minutes. Cool completely on wire racks. Melt over hot (not boiling) water, remaining 1 cup Nestlé Toll House mint-chocolate morsels; stir until smooth. Spread flat side of each cookie with ½ slightly rounded teaspoonful melted morsels. Chill until set.

*Mixture will appear curdled.

Minty Fudge Brownies

Makes 4 dozen 1½-inch brownies

  1¼ cups all-purpose flour
  ½ teaspoon baking soda
  ½ teaspoon salt
  1 cup sugar
  ½ cup butter
  3 tablespoons water
One 10-ounce package (1½ cups) Nestlé Toll House
    mint-chocolate morsels
  1½ teaspoons vanilla extract
  3 eggs
  1 cup chopped nuts
  Walnut halves (optional)

Preheat oven to 325°F. In small bowl, combine flour, baking soda and salt; set aside. In medium saucepan, combine sugar, butter and water; bring *just to a boil*. Remove from heat. Add Nestlé Toll House mint-chocolate morsels and vanilla extract; stir until morsels are melted and mixture is smooth. Transfer to large bowl. Add eggs, 1 at a time, beating well after each addition. Gradually blend in flour mixture. Stir in nuts. Spread into greased 13×9-inch baking pan. Bake at 325°F. for 30–35 minutes. Cool completely on wire rack; cut into 1½-inch squares. Garnish with walnut halves, if desired.

Minty Fudge Brownies (top)
Black & White Cheesecake Brownies (bottom)

Maple Walnut Bars

Makes 4½ dozen 2×1-inch bars

1 cup all-purpose flour
½ teaspoon baking powder
½ cup butter, softened
½ cup firmly packed brown sugar
1 egg
½ cup maple flavored syrup
1 teaspoon vanilla extract
One 12-ounce package (2 cups) Nestlé Toll House
   Little Bits semi-sweet chocolate, divided
1 cup finely chopped walnuts, divided

Preheat oven to 350°F. In small bowl, combine flour and baking powder; set aside. In large bowl, combine butter and brown sugar; beat until creamy. Add egg, maple flavored syrup and vanilla extract; beat well. Gradually beat in flour mixture. Stir in 1 cup Nestlé Toll House Little Bits semi-sweet chocolate and ⅔ cup walnuts. Spread into greased 13×9-inch baking pan. Bake at 350°F. for 25 minutes. Remove from oven; immediately sprinkle with remaining 1 cup Nestlé Toll House Little Bits semi-sweet chocolate. Let stand about 3 minutes until morsels become shiny and soft; spread evenly over top of bars. Sprinkle with remaining ⅓ cup walnuts. Cool completely on wire rack. Cut into 2×1-inch bars.

Chocolate Raspberry Coconut Squares

Chocolate Raspberry Coconut Squares

Makes 3 dozen 1½-inch squares

COOKIE BASE:
1 cup all-purpose flour
¼ cup firmly packed brown sugar
½ cup butter, softened

TOPPING:
1 cup sweetened condensed milk
½ cup all-purpose flour
½ teaspoon baking powder
¼ teaspoon salt
2 eggs
One 6-ounce package (1 cup) Nestlé Toll House
   semi-sweet chocolate morsels
One 3½-ounce can (1⅓ cups) flaked coconut,
   divided
½ cup chopped pecans
½ cup raspberry preserves

Cookie Base: Preheat oven to 350°F. In medium bowl, combine flour and brown sugar. With pastry blender or 2 knives, cut in butter until mixture resembles fine crumbs. Press into greased 9-inch square baking pan. Bake at 350°F. for 20 minutes.

Topping: In large bowl, combine sweetened condensed milk, flour, baking powder, salt and eggs; mix well. Stir in Nestlé Toll House semi-sweet chocolate morsels, 1 cup coconut and pecans. Pour over baked Cookie Base. Bake at 350°F. for 25 minutes. Remove from oven. Spread preserves over top of bars. Sprinkle with remaining ⅓ cup coconut. Cool completely on wire rack. Cut into 1½-inch squares.

Magic Cookie Bars

Makes 4½ dozen 2×1-inch bars

½ cup butter
1½ cups graham cracker crumbs
One 14-ounce can sweetened condensed milk
One 6-ounce package (1 cup) Nestlé Toll House
   semi-sweet chocolate morsels
One 3½-ounce can (1⅓ cups) flaked coconut
1 cup chopped walnuts

Preheat oven to 350°F. In 13×9-inch baking pan, melt butter in oven. Remove from oven; add graham cracker crumbs. Mix well and press into pan. Pour sweetened condensed milk evenly over crumbs. Sprinkle Nestlé Toll House semi-sweet chocolate morsels, coconut and walnuts on top; press down firmly. Bake at 350°F. for 25–30 minutes. Cool completely on wire rack. Cut into 2×1-inch bars.

Butterscotch Granola Cookies

Butterscotch Granola Cookies

Makes about 5 dozen 2¼-inch cookies

1½ cups all-purpose flour
 1 teaspoon cinnamon
 ½ teaspoon salt
 ½ teaspoon baking powder
 ½ teaspoon baking soda
 ½ cup butter, softened
 ½ cup honey
 ½ cup firmly packed brown sugar
 1 egg
 1 teaspoon vanilla extract
 ¼ cup milk
One 12-ounce package (2 cups) Nestlé Toll House
      butterscotch flavored morsels
 1 cup quick oats, uncooked
 1 cup chopped walnuts
 ¾ cup raisins
 ¼ cup wheat germm

Preheat oven to 350°F. In small bowl, combine flour, cinnamon, salt, baking powder and baking soda; set aside. In large bowl, combine butter, honey and brown sugar; beat until creamy. Beat in egg and vanilla extract. Blend in flour mixture alternately with milk. Stir in Nestlé Toll House butterscotch flavored morsels, oats, walnuts, raisins and wheat germ. Drop by rounded teaspoonfuls onto greased cookie sheets. Bake at 350°F. for 8–10 minutes. Allow to stand 2 minutes; remove from cookie sheets. Cool completely on wire racks.

(continued)

Oatmeal Scotchies™

Makes about 4 dozen 3-inch cookies

1 cup all-purpose flour
1 teaspoon baking soda
½ teaspoon salt
½ teaspoon cinnamon
1 cup butter, softened
¾ cup sugar
¾ cup firmly packed brown sugar
2 eggs
1 teaspoon vanilla extract
3 cups oats, uncooked (Quick or Old Fashioned)
One 12-ounce package (2 cups) Nestlé Toll House butterscotch flavored morsels

Preheat oven to 375°F. In small bowl, combine flour, baking soda, salt and cinnamon; set aside. In large bowl, combine butter, sugar, brown sugar, eggs and vanilla extract; beat until creamy. Gradually add flour mixture. Stir in oats and Nestlé Toll House butterscotch flavored morsels. Drop by level tablespoonfuls onto ungreased cookie sheets. Bake at 375°F. for 7–8 minutes for chewier cookies, 9–10 minutes for crisper cookies.

Oatmeal Scotchie Pan Cookie: Spread the dough into greased 15½×10½×1-inch baking pan. Bake at 375°F. for 20–25 minutes. Cool completely. Cut into thirty-five 2-inch squares.

Mocha Walnut Cookies

Makes about 2 dozen 3-inch cookies

One 12-ounce package (2 cups) Nestlé Toll House semi-sweet chocolate morsels, divided
2 tablespoons Nescafé Classic instant coffee
2 teaspoons boiling water
1¼ cups all-purpose flour
¾ teaspoon baking soda
½ teaspoon salt
½ cup butter, softened
½ cup sugar
½ cup firmly packed brown sugar
1 egg
½ cup chopped walnuts

(continued)

Preheat oven to 350°F. Melt over hot (not boiling) water, ½ cup Nestlé Toll House semi-sweet chocolate morsels; stir until smooth. Cool to room temperature. In small cup, dissolve Nescafé Classic instant coffee in boiling water; set aside. In small bowl, combine flour, baking soda and salt; set aside. In large bowl, combine butter, sugar, brown sugar and coffee; beat until creamy. Add egg and melted morsels; mix well. Gradually beat in flour mixture. Stir in remaining 1½ cups Nestlé Toll House semi-sweet chocolate morsels and walnuts. Drop by rounded tablespoonfuls onto ungreased cookie sheets. Bake at 350°F. for 10–12 minutes. Allow to stand 2–3 minutes before removing from cookie sheets; cool completely on wire racks.

Butterscotch Lemon Cookies

Makes about 1½ dozen 3-inch cookies

1½ cups all-purpose flour
2 teaspoons baking powder
½ teaspoon salt
¾ cup sugar
½ cup butter, softened
1 egg
2 tablespoons milk
1 tablespoon lemon juice
1 teaspoon grated lemon rind
¾ of 12-ounce package (1½ cups) Nestlé Toll House butterscotch flavored morsels

Preheat oven to 375°F. In small bowl, combine flour, baking powder and salt; set aside. In large bowl, combine sugar and butter; beat well. Add egg, milk, lemon juice and lemon rind; beat well.* Gradually beat in flour mixture. Stir in Nestlé Toll House butterscotch flavored morsels. Drop by rounded tablespoonfuls onto greased cookie sheets. Bake at 375°F. for 8–10 minutes. Allow to stand 2 minutes before removing from cookie sheets. Cool completely on wire racks.

Mixture will appear curdled.

Oatmeal Scotchies™
Butterscotch Lemon Cookies

No-Bake Butterscotch Snack Bars

Makes 4½ dozen 2×1-inch bars

**One 14-ounce box circle shaped bran cereal,
 coarsely crushed
1 cup raisins
⅔ cup corn syrup
3 tablespoons butter
½ of 12-ounce package (1 cup) Nestlé Toll House
 butterscotch flavored morsels**

In large bowl, combine cereal and raisins; set aside. In heavy gauge saucepan, combine corn syrup and butter. Bring to *full rolling boil* over medium heat, stirring occasionally. Remove from heat. Add Nestlé Toll House butterscotch flavored morsels; stir until morsels are melted and mixture is smooth. Pour over cereal; mix well. Press into foil-lined 13×9-inch pan. Chill until set (about 10 minutes). Cut into 2×1-inch bars.

Chocolate Cinnabar Wreaths

Makes about 7½ dozen 2-inch cookies

**One 6-ounce package (1 cup) Nestlé Toll House
 semi-sweet chocolate morsels
1 cup butter, softened
⅔ cup sugar
1 teaspoon vanilla extract
2 eggs
2½ cups all-purpose flour
One 4-ounce jar cinnamon candies**

Melt over hot (not boiling) water, Nestlé Toll House semi-sweet chocolate morsels; stir until smooth. Remove from heat; set aside. In large bowl, combine butter, sugar and vanilla extract; beat until creamy. Add eggs; beat well. Stir in melted morsels. Gradually beat in flour. Cover dough; chill 30–45 minutes. Preheat oven to 400°F. Place dough in cookie press. Use star tip to shape cookies into 2-inch circles. Place cinnamon candies on each cookie. Bake at 400°F. for 5 minutes. Cool completely on wire racks.

No-Bake Butterscotch Snack Bars

Chocolate-Dipped Brandy Snaps

Chocolate-Dipped Brandy Snaps

Makes about 3 dozen 2½-inch snaps

½ cup butter
½ cup sugar
⅓ cup dark corn syrup
½ teaspoon cinnamon
¼ teaspoon ginger
1 cup all-purpose flour
2 teaspoons brandy
One 6-ounce package (1 cup) Nestlé Toll House
    semi-sweet chocolate morsels
1 tablespoon vegetable shortening
⅓ cup finely chopped nuts   *(continued)*

Preheat oven to 300°F. In heavy gauge saucepan, combine butter, sugar, dark corn syrup, cinnamon and ginger; cook over medium heat, stirring constantly, until melted and smooth. Remove from heat; stir in flour and brandy. Drop by rounded teaspoonfuls onto ungreased cookie sheets about 3 inches apart. (Do *not* bake more than 6 cookies at one time.) Bake at 300°F. for 10–12 minutes. Let stand a few seconds. Remove from cookie sheets and immediately roll around wooden spoon handle; cool completely. Combine over hot (not boiling) water, Nestlé Toll House semi-sweet chocolate morsels and vegetable shortening; stir until morsels are melted and mixture is smooth. Dip Brandy Snap halfway in melted chocolate. Sprinkle with nuts; set on waxed-paper-lined cookie sheets. Chill until set. Store in airtight container in refrigerator.

Chocolate Orange Granola Cookies

Makes about 1½ dozen 2-inch cookies

  1 cup all-purpose flour
  ½ teaspoon baking powder
  ½ teaspoon allspice
  ½ teaspoon salt
  ⅔ cup firmly packed brown sugar
  ½ cup butter, softened
  1 egg
  1 teaspoon vanilla extract
  ½ teaspoon grated orange rind
  1¼ cups granola cereal
One 6-ounce package (1 cup) Nestlé Toll House
      semi-sweet chocolate morsels
  ½ cup flaked coconut
  ¼ cup chopped nuts

Preheat oven to 350°F. In small bowl, combine flour, baking powder, allspice and salt; set aside. In large bowl, combine brown sugar and butter; beat until creamy. Add egg, vanilla extract and orange rind; beat well. Gradually beat in flour mixture. Stir in granola cereal, Nestlé Toll House semi-sweet chocolate morsels, coconut and nuts. Drop by rounded tablespoonfuls onto ungreased cookie sheets. Sprinkle with additional coconut, if desired. Bake at 350°F. for 9–11 minutes. Cool completely on wire racks.

No-Bake Fudge Brownies

Makes sixteen 2-inch brownies

One 12-ounce package (2 cups) Nestlé Toll House
      semi-sweet chocolate morsels
One 14-ounce can sweetened condensed milk
One 8½-ounce package chocolate wafers, finely
      crushed
  1 cup chopped nuts, divided

Melt over hot (not boiling) water, Nestlé Toll House semi-sweet chocolate morsels; stir until smooth. Add sweetened condensed milk, chocolate wafer crumbs and ½ cup nuts; stir until well blended. Press into foil-lined 8-inch square pan. Press remaining ½ cup nuts into top of brownie. Let stand at room temperature until firm. Cut into 2-inch squares.

Double Chocolate Cookies

Makes about 6 dozen 2½-inch cookies

  2¼ cups all-purpose flour
  1 teaspoon baking soda
  1 teaspoon salt
  1 cup butter, softened
  ¾ cup sugar
  ¾ cup firmly packed brown sugar
  1 teaspoon vanilla extract
  2 eggs
Two envelopes (2 ounces) Nestlé Choco-bake
      unsweetened baking chocolate flavor
One 12-ounce package (2 cups) Nestlé Toll House
      semi-sweet chocolate morsels
  1 cup chopped walnuts

Preheat oven to 375°F. In medium bowl, combine flour, baking soda and salt; set aside. In large bowl, combine butter, sugar, brown sugar and vanilla extract; beat until creamy. Beat in eggs and Nestlé Choco-bake unsweetened baking chocolate flavor. Gradually beat in flour mixture. Stir in Nestlé Toll House semi-sweet chocolate morsels and nuts. Drop by rounded teaspoonfuls onto ungreased cookie sheets. Bake at 375°F. for 8–10 minutes. Cool completely on wire racks.

Spice Islands Butterscotch Bars

Makes 4½ dozen 2×1-inch bars

  1¾ cups all-purpose flour
  1 teaspoon ground ginger
  ½ teaspoon baking soda
  ¼ teaspoon ground cloves
  ¾ cup + 2 tablespoons vegetable oil
  ½ cup molasses
  ¼ cup firmly packed brown sugar
  1 egg
  1 cup chopped nuts
  ½ of 12-ounce package (1 cup) Nestlé Toll House
      butterscotch flavored morsels
  Confectioners' sugar

Preheat oven to 350°F. In small bowl, combine flour, ginger, baking soda and cloves; set aside. In large bowl, combine vegetable oil, molasses, brown sugar and egg; beat well. Gradually beat in flour mixture. Stir in nuts and Nestlé Toll House butterscotch flavored morsels. Pour into greased 13×9-inch baking pan. Bake at 350°F. for 20–25 minutes. Cool completely on wire rack. Sprinkle with confectioners' sugar. Cut into 2×1-inch bars.

Double Chocolate Cookies
Chocolate Orange Granola Cookies

Chocolate-Dipped Sandwich Macaroons

Makes about 4 dozen 1½-inch cookies

**One 12-ounce package (2 cups) Nestlé Toll House
    Little Bits semi-sweet chocolate, divided
1½ cups blanched almonds, finely ground
1½ cups sifted confectioners' sugar
  3 egg whites, at room temperature
  ⅓ cup jam or jelly
  2 tablespoons vegetable shortening**

Preheat oven to 350°F. In small bowl, combine 1 cup
Nestlé Toll House Little Bits semi-sweet chocolate,
almonds and confectioners' sugar; set aside. In large
bowl, beat egg whites until stiff peaks form. Fold in
almond mixture. Drop by level teaspoonfuls onto
parchment-paper-lined cookie sheets. Bake at 350°F.
for 8–10 minutes. Cool 5 minutes. Remove from paper
to wire racks; cool completely. Spread ¼ teaspoon jam
or jelly on flat side of one cookie; top with second
cookie. Repeat with remaining cookies. Set aside.
Combine over hot (not boiling) water, remaining 1 cup
Nestlé Toll House Little Bits semi-sweet chocolate and
vegetable shortening. Stir until morsels are melted
and mixture is smooth. Remove from heat, but keep
over hot water. Dip ½ of each sandwich cookie into
chocolate. Place on waxed-paper-lined cookie sheets.
Chill until set.

Chocolate-Dipped Sandwich Macaroons

Cappuccino Brownies

Makes sixteen 2-inch brownies

**1 tablespoon Taster's Choice Maragor Bold freeze
    dried coffee
2 teaspoons boiling water
One 6-ounce package (1 cup) Nestlé Toll House
    semi-sweet chocolate morsels
  ½ cup sugar
  ¼ cup butter, softened
  2 eggs
  ¼ teaspoon cinnamon
  ½ cup all-purpose flour**

Preheat oven to 350°F. In cup, combine Taster's Choice
Maragor Bold freeze dried coffee and water; set aside.
Melt over hot (not boiling) water, Nestlé Toll House
semi-sweet chocolate morsels; stir until smooth. Set
aside. In large bowl, combine sugar and butter; beat
until creamy. Add eggs, coffee and cinnamon; beat
well. Stir in melted morsels and flour. Spread into foil-
lined 8-inch square baking pan. Bake at 350°F. for 25–
30 minutes. Cool completely on wire rack. Cut into 2-
inch squares.

Chocolate Macaroon Squares

Makes 2 dozen 2-inch squares

**TOPPING:
One 14-ounce can sweetened condensed milk
  1 teaspoon vanilla extract
  1 egg
One 3½-ounce can (1⅓ cups) flaked coconut,
    divided
  1 cup chopped pecans
One 6-ounce package (1 cup) Nestlé Toll House
    semi-sweet chocolate morsels**

**BASE:
One 18½-ounce package chocolate cake mix
  ⅓ cup butter, softened
  1 egg**

Topping: In large bowl, combine sweetened
condensed milk, vanilla extract and egg; beat until well
blended. Stir in 1 cup coconut, pecans and Nestlé Toll
House semi-sweet chocolate morsels. Set aside.

Base: Preheat oven to 350°F. In large bowl, combine
cake mix, butter and egg; mix until crumbly. Press into
greased 13×9-inch baking pan.

Spread Topping over Base. Sprinkle remaining ⅓ cup
coconut on top. Bake at 350°F. for 30–40 minutes.
NOTE: Center may appear loose but will set upon
cooling. Cool completely on wire rack. Cut into 2-inch
squares.

Chocolate Macaroon Squares (top)
Cappuccino Brownies (bottom)

Chocolate Mint Cookies (left); Chocolate Mint Meltaways (right)

Chocolate Mint Cookies

Makes about 3½ dozen 2-inch cookies

COOKIES:
One 10-ounce package (1½ cups) Nestlé Toll House
    mint-chocolate morsels, divided
  1 cup all-purpose flour
  ¾ teaspoon baking powder
  ¼ teaspoon baking soda
  ¼ teaspoon salt
  ¼ cup butter, softened
  6 tablespoons sugar
  ½ teaspoon vanilla extract
  1 egg

GLAZE:
  1 cup Nestlé Toll House mint-chocolate morsels,
    reserved from 10-ounce package
  ¼ cup vegetable shortening
  3 tablespoons corn syrup
  2¼ teaspoons water   *(continued)*

Cookies: Melt over hot (not boiling) water, ½ cup Nestlé Toll House mint-chocolate morsels; stir until smooth. Set aside. In small bowl, combine flour, baking powder, baking soda and salt; set aside. In large bowl, combine butter, sugar and vanilla extract; beat until creamy. Beat in egg; blend in melted morsels. Gradually beat in flour mixture. Shape dough into ball and wrap in waxed paper. Chill about 1 hour. Preheat oven to 350°F. On lightly floured board, roll dough to ³⁄₁₆-inch thickness. Cut with 2-inch cookie cutter. Reroll remaining dough and cut out cookies. Place on ungreased cookie sheets. Bake at 350°F. for 8–10 minutes. Cool completely on wire racks.

Glaze: Combine over hot (not boiling) water, remaining 1 cup Nestlé Toll House mint-chocolate morsels, vegetable shortening, corn syrup and water; stir until morsels are melted and mixture is smooth. Remove from heat, but keep mixture over hot water.

Dip ½ of each cookie into Glaze; shake off any excess Glaze. Place cookies on waxed-paper-lined cookie sheets. Chill until Glaze sets (about 10 minutes).

Note: Keep refrigerated until ready to serve.

Chocolate Mint Meltaways

Makes about 4 dozen 1¾-inch cookies

COOKIES:
One 10-ounce package (1½ cups) Nestlé Toll House
    mint-chocolate morsels, divided
¾ cup butter, softened
½ cup sifted confectioners' sugar
1 egg yolk
1¼ cups all-purpose flour

GLAZE:
½ cup Nestlé Toll House mint-chocolate morsels,
    reserved from 10-ounce package
1½ tablespoons vegetable shortening

2 tablespoons chopped toasted almonds

Cookies: Preheat oven to 350°F. Melt over hot (not boiling) water, 1 cup Nestlé Toll House mint-chocolate morsels; stir until smooth. Set aside. In large bowl, combine butter, confectioners' sugar and egg yolk; beat until creamy. Add melted morsels and flour; beat until well blended. Drop by heaping teaspoonfuls onto ungreased cookie sheets. Bake at 350°F. for 8–10 minutes. Allow to stand 3 minutes before removing from cookie sheets. Cool completely on wire racks.

Glaze: Combine over hot (not boiling) water, remaining ½ cup Nestlé Toll House mint-chocolate morsels and vegetable shortening. Stir until morsels are melted and mixture is smooth.

Drizzle each cookie with ½ teaspoon Glaze; sprinkle with almonds. Chill until set. Store in airtight container in refrigerator.

Little Bits™ Meringue Wreaths

Makes about 2½ dozen cookies

2 egg whites
¼ teaspoon cream of tartar
⅓ cup sugar
¼ of 12-ounce package (½ cup) Nestlé Toll House
    Little Bits semi-sweet chocolate
One 3-ounce package candied cherries, cut in
    quarters

Preheat oven to 275°F. In 1½-quart bowl, combine egg whites and cream of tartar; beat until soft peaks form. Gradually add sugar; beat until stiff peaks form. Fold in Nestlé Toll House Little Bits semi-sweet chocolate. Spoon into pastry bag fitted with rounded #7 pastry tip. Pipe 2-inch circles onto parchment-paper-lined cookie sheets. Top each with 2 candied cherry pieces. Bake at 275°F. for 20 minutes. Turn oven off; leave in oven with door ajar 30 minutes. Cool completely on wire racks; remove from paper. Store in airtight container.

Anise Cookie Cordials

Makes about 4¼ dozen 1-inch cookies

2¾ cups all-purpose flour
1½ teaspoons baking powder
1 cup sugar
½ cup butter, softened
3 eggs
2 tablespoons anise flavored liqueur
2 tablespoons water
1 tablespoon anise seed
½ of 12-ounce package (1 cup) Nestlé Toll House
    Little Bits semi-sweet chocolate
1 cup coarsely chopped toasted almonds

In medium bowl, combine flour and baking powder; set aside. In large bowl, combine sugar and butter; beat until creamy. Add eggs, anise flavored liqueur, water and anise seed; beat until well blended. Gradually beat in flour mixture. Stir in Nestlé Toll House Little Bits semi-sweet chocolate and almonds. Cover; chill several hours. Preheat oven to 375°F. Divide dough into 4 pieces. With floured hands, shape each piece into 15½×2×½-inch loaf. Place loaves 4 inches apart on greased cookie sheets. Bake at 375°F. for 15 minutes. Remove from oven. Cut into 1-inch slices. Place slices back on cookie sheets. Bake at 375°F. for 7 minutes. Turn cookies over. Bake at 375°F. for 7 minutes. Cool completely on wire racks.

Anise Cookie Cordials

Chocolate Mint Sugar Cookie Drops

Makes about 5½ dozen 2-inch cookies

2½ cups all-purpose flour
1½ teaspoons baking powder
¾ teaspoon salt
1¼ cups sugar, divided
¾ cup vegetable oil
2 eggs
1 teaspoon vanilla extract
One 10-ounce package (1½ cups) Nestlé Toll House mint-chocolate morsels

In medium bowl, combine flour, baking powder and salt; set aside. In large bowl, combine 1 cup sugar and vegetable oil; mix well. Beat in eggs and vanilla extract. Gradually beat in flour mixture. Stir in Nestlé Toll House mint-chocolate morsels. Shape into balls using rounded teaspoonfuls of dough; roll in remaining ¼ cup sugar. Place on ungreased cookie sheets. Bake at 350°F. for 8–10 minutes. Cool completely on wire racks.

Double Chocolate Mint Chip Cookies

Makes about 1½ dozen 2-inch cookies

One 10-ounce package (1½ cups) Nestlé Toll House mint-chocolate morsels, divided
1¼ cups all-purpose flour
¾ teaspoon baking soda
½ teaspoon salt
½ cup butter, softened
½ cup firmly packed brown sugar
¼ cup sugar
½ teaspoon vanilla extract
1 egg
½ cup chopped nuts

Preheat oven to 375°F. Melt over hot (not boiling) water, ¾ cup Nestlé Toll House mint-chocolate morsels; stir until smooth. Remove from heat; cool to room temperature. In small bowl, combine flour, baking soda and salt; set aside. In large bowl, combine butter, brown sugar, sugar and vanilla extract; beat until creamy. Add melted morsels and egg; beat well. Gradually blend in flour mixture. Stir in remaining ¾ cup Nestlé Toll House mint-chocolate morsels and nuts. Drop by rounded tablespoonfuls onto ungreased cookie sheets. Bake at 375°F. for 8–9 minutes. Allow to stand 2–3 minutes; remove from cookie sheets. Cool completely on wire racks.

Chocolate Mint Sugar Cookie Drops
Double Chocolate Mint Chip Cookies

Mocha Shortbread Cookies

Makes about 1½ dozen 2½-inch cookies

1 teaspoon Nescafé Classic instant coffee
1 teaspoon boiling water
One 12-ounce package (2 cups) Nestlé Toll House semi-sweet chocolate morsels, divided
¾ cup butter, softened
1¼ cups sifted confectioners' sugar
1 cup all-purpose flour
⅛ teaspoon salt

Preheat oven to 250°F. In cup, dissolve Nescafé Classic instant coffee in boiling water; set aside. Melt over hot (not boiling) water, 1 cup Nestlé Toll House semi-sweet chocolate morsels; stir until smooth. Remove from heat; set aside. In large bowl, combine butter, confectioners' sugar and coffee; beat until smooth. Gradually blend in flour and salt. Stir in melted morsels. Roll dough between two pieces of waxed paper to ³⁄₁₆-inch thickness. Remove top sheet; cut out cookies using 2½-inch cookie cutter. Remove from waxed paper and place on ungreased cookie sheets. Bake at 250°F. for 25 minutes. Cool completely on wire racks. Melt over hot (not boiling) water, remaining 1 cup Nestlé Toll House semi-sweet chocolate morsels; stir until smooth. Spread slightly rounded teaspoonful of melted chocolate on flat side of cookie; top with second cookie. Repeat with remaining cookies. Chill until set. Let stand at room temperature 15 minutes before serving.

Irish Coffee Brownies

Makes sixteen 2-inch brownies

One 11½-ounce package (2 cups) Nestlé Toll House milk chocolate morsels, divided
½ cup butter
½ cup sugar
2 eggs
1 teaspoon vanilla extract
2 tablespoons Irish whiskey
2 teaspoons Nescafé Classic instant coffee
1 cup all-purpose flour

Preheat oven to 350°F. In small saucepan over low heat, combine 1 cup Nestlé Toll House milk chocolate morsels and butter; stir until morsels are melted and mixture is smooth. Cool to room temperature. In large bowl, combine sugar and eggs; beat until thick and lemon colored. Gradually beat in chocolate mixture and vanilla extract. In cup, combine Irish whiskey and Nescafé Classic instant coffee; stir until dissolved. Add to chocolate mixture. Gradually blend in flour. Pour into foil-lined 8-inch square baking pan. Bake at 350°F. for 25–30 minutes. Immediately sprinkle remaining 1 cup Nestlé Toll House milk chocolate morsels on top. Let stand until morsels are shiny and soft; spread evenly. Cool completely on wire rack; cut into 2-inch squares.

Milk Chocolate Florentine Cookies

Milk Chocolate Florentine Cookies

Makes about 3½ dozen sandwich cookies

⅔ cup butter
2 cups quick oats, uncooked
1 cup sugar
⅔ cup all-purpose flour
¼ cup corn syrup
¼ cup milk
1 teaspoon vanilla extract
¼ teaspoon salt
One 11½-ounce package (2 cups) Nestlé Toll House
    milk chocolate morsels   *(continued)*

Preheat oven to 375°F. Melt butter in medium saucepan over low heat. Remove from heat. Stir in oats, sugar, flour, corn syrup, milk, vanilla extract and salt; mix well. Drop by level teaspoonfuls, about 3 inches apart, onto foil-lined cookie sheets. Spread thin with rubber spatula. Bake at 375°F. for 5–7 minutes. Cool completely on wire racks. Peel foil away from cookies. Melt over hot (not boiling) water, Nestlé Toll House milk chocolate morsels; stir until smooth. Spread chocolate on flat side of ½ the cookies. Top with remaining cookies.

Chocolate Date Envelopes

Makes about 2 dozen 2½-inch cookies

COOKIES:
1¼ cups all-purpose flour
One 3-ounce package cream cheese, softened
½ cup butter, softened

FILLING:
½ of 12-ounce package (1 cup) Nestlé Toll House
   Little Bits semi-sweet chocolate
One 8-ounce package pitted dates, chopped
½ cup finely chopped walnuts
2 teaspoons grated orange rind
2 teaspoons orange juice
Confectioners' sugar

Cookies: In medium bowl, combine flour, cream cheese and butter; knead until well blended. Shape into ball; wrap in plastic wrap and chill.

Filling: In medium bowl, combine Nestlé Toll House Little Bits semi-sweet chocolate, dates, walnuts, orange rind and juice. Press into ball. Preheat oven to 350°F. On floured board, roll dough into 12½-inch square; cut into 2½-inch squares. Shape rounded teaspoonful Filling into log. Place in center of square. Bring two diagonal corners of each square to the center and pinch. Place on ungreased cookie sheets. Bake at 350°F. for 20 minutes. Cool completely on wire racks. Sprinkle with confectioners' sugar.

Oatmeal Extravaganzas

Makes 3 dozen 1½-inch squares

1 cup + 2 tablespoons all-purpose flour
1½ teaspoons baking powder
½ teaspoon salt
1 cup + 2 tablespoons firmly packed brown sugar
¾ cup butter, softened
2 teaspoons vanilla extract
¼ cup water
2 cups quick oats, uncooked
One 12-ounce package (2 cups) Nestlé Toll House
   semi-sweet chocolate morsels

Preheat oven to 375°F. In small bowl, combine flour, baking powder and salt; set aside. In large bowl, combine brown sugar, butter and vanilla extract; beat until creamy. Gradually blend in flour mixture alternately with water. Stir in oats and Nestlé Toll House semi-sweet chocolate morsels. Spread in greased 9-inch square baking pan. Bake at 375°F. for 30 minutes. Cool completely on wire racks; cut into 1½-inch squares.

Chocolate Almond Macaroons

Makes 2 dozen 2-inch cookies

COOKIES:
One 12-ounce package (2 cups) Nestlé Toll House
   Little Bits semi-sweet chocolate, divided
2 egg whites
One 8-ounce can almond paste
⅓ cup sifted confectioners' sugar
2 tablespoons all-purpose flour

TOPPING:
1 cup Nestlé Toll House Little Bits semi-sweet
   chocolate, reserved from 12-ounce package,
   divided
1 tablespoon vegetable shortening
¼ cup chopped blanched almonds

Cookies: Preheat oven to 300°F. Melt over hot (not boiling) water, 1 cup Nestlé Toll House Little Bits semi-sweet chocolate; stir until smooth. Set aside. In large bowl, combine egg whites, almond paste, confectioners' sugar and flour; beat until smooth. Blend in melted chocolate. Spoon macaroon mixture into pastry bag fitted with rosette tip. Pipe 1¾-inch rosettes onto foil-lined cookie sheets. Bake at 300°F. for 25 minutes. Cool completely on wire racks.

Topping: Combine over hot (not boiling) water, ¾ cup Nestlé Toll House Little Bits semi-sweet chocolate and vegetable shortening; stir until morsels are melted and mixture is smooth. Drizzle each macaroon with ½ rounded teaspoonful of chocolate. Sprinkle with remaining ¼ cup Nestlé Little Bits semi-sweet chocolate and chopped almonds.

Chocolate Almond Macaroons (top)
Chocolate Date Envelopes (bottom)

PIES

Chocolate Chip Tarts à l'Orange

Makes 12 tarts

One 15-ounce container ricotta cheese
2 eggs
¼ cup sugar
2 tablespoons butter, melted
½ teaspoon vanilla extract
One 6-ounce package (1 cup) Nestlé Toll House
    semi-sweet chocolate morsels
Two 4-ounce packages single serve graham crusts
Two 11-ounce cans mandarin oranges, drained
¼ cup apricot preserves

Preheat oven to 350°F. In large bowl, combine ricotta cheese, eggs, sugar, butter and vanilla extract; beat well. Stir in Nestlé Toll House semi-sweet chocolate morsels. Spoon ¼ cup into each crust. Place on cookie sheet. Bake at 350°F. for 20–25 minutes. Centers will be soft. Cool completely. Arrange orange segments on top of each tart. In small saucepan over low heat, melt apricot preserves. Brush orange segments with preserves. Chill.

Minty Mousse Pie au Chocolat

Makes one 9-inch pie

6 tablespoons sugar, divided
2 tablespoons + 2 teaspoons cornstarch
⅔ of 10-ounce package (1 cup) Nestlé Toll House
    mint-chocolate morsels
1½ cups milk
1 cup heavy cream
One 9-inch prepared graham cracker crust

(continued)

In medium heavy gauge saucepan, combine 4 tablespoons sugar, cornstarch and Nestlé Toll House mint-chocolate morsels. Gradually stir in milk. Cook, stirring constantly, over medium heat until mixture *boils*. *Boil 1 minute*; remove from heat. Transfer to large bowl; cover surface of chocolate mixture with plastic wrap. Cool to room temperature (20–30 minutes). In medium bowl, combine heavy cream with remaining 2 tablespoons sugar; beat until stiff. Remove plastic wrap from chocolate; beat well. Fold in whipped cream. Spoon into crust. Chill until firm (about 2–3 hours).

Nutty Chocolate Sour Cream Pie

Makes one 9-inch pie

4 eggs
⅔ cup sour cream
⅔ cup firmly packed brown sugar
¼ cup honey
1 teaspoon vanilla extract
2 cups chopped pecans
One 6-ounce package (1 cup) Nestlé Toll House
    semi-sweet chocolate morsels
One 9-inch unbaked pie shell*
    Whipped cream (optional)

Preheat oven to 350°F. In large bowl, combine eggs, sour cream, brown sugar, honey and vanilla extract; beat well. Stir in pecans and Nestlé Toll House semi-sweet chocolate morsels. Pour into prepared pie shell.* Bake at 350°F. for 40–45 minutes. Serve warm with whipped cream, if desired.

**If using frozen pie shell, it's necessary to use deep dish style, thawed. Place on cookie sheet and bake additional 10 minutes.*

Chocolate Cream Strawberry Tart

Chocolate Cream Strawberry Tart

Makes one 9-inch tart

TART SHELL:
  Pastry for one crust 9-inch pie

PASTRY CREAM:
  ¼ cup sugar
  3 tablespoons all-purpose flour
  ¼ teaspoon salt
  1 cup milk
  4 egg yolks
One 6-ounce package (1 cup) Nestlé Toll House
      semi-sweet chocolate morsels
  2 tablespoons butter
  2 teaspoons vanilla extract
  2 pints strawberries, washed and hulled
  2 tablespoons strawberry jelly   (continued)

Tart Shell: Preheat oven to 425°F. Fit pastry dough into 9-inch removable-bottom tart pan. Press dough firmly into bottom and sides of pan; trim edges. Line pastry dough with foil; weight with dried beans. Bake at 425°F. for 10 minutes. Remove foil; bake additional 2–3 minutes. Cool completely. Remove from pan.

Pastry Cream: In medium saucepan, combine sugar, flour and salt. Gradually add milk. Cook over low heat, stirring constantly, until mixture *boils*. Boil 2 *minutes*, stirring constantly; remove from heat. Beat in egg yolks; return to heat and cook 1 minute longer. Remove from heat. Add Nestlé Toll House semi-sweet chocolate morsels, butter and vanilla extract. Stir until morsels are melted and mixture is smooth. Place plastic wrap on surface of pastry cream. Chill 30 minutes. Stir; spread evenly into baked Tart Shell. Arrange strawberries on top. In small saucepan over low heat, melt strawberry jelly. Brush over strawberries. Chill several hours. Let stand at room temperature 15 minutes before serving.

Butterscotch Crumb Apple Pie

Butterscotch Crumb Apple Pie

Makes one 9-inch pie

FILLING:
    4 cups pared, cored and sliced tart cooking
      apples
1½ teaspoons lemon juice
  ½ cup sugar
  ¼ cup all-purpose flour
  1 teaspoon cinnamon
  ⅛ teaspoon salt
One 9-inch unbaked pie shell*

TOPPING:
  ½ of 12-ounce package (1 cup) Nestlé Toll House
      butterscotch flavored morsels
  ¼ cup butter
  ¾ cup all-purpose flour
  ⅛ teaspoon salt
     Whipped cream or ice cream (optional)

(continued)

Filling: Preheat oven to 375°F. In large bowl, combine apples and lemon juice; toss until well coated. Stir in sugar, flour, cinnamon and salt; mix well. Spoon into pie shell.* Cover edges with aluminum foil. Bake at 375°F. for 20 minutes.

Topping: Combine over hot (not boiling) water, Nestlé Toll House butterscotch flavored morsels and butter; stir until morsels are melted and mixture is smooth. Remove from heat. Add flour and salt; blend until mixture forms large crumbs. Remove foil from pie. Crumble Topping over hot apples. Bake at 375°F. for 25 minutes longer. Serve warm with whipped cream or ice cream, if desired.

If using frozen pie shell, it's necessary to use deep dish style, thawed. Place on cookie sheet and bake additional 10 minutes.

Classic Mud Pie

Makes one 9-inch pie

CHOCOLATE COOKIE CRUST:
One 12-ounce package (2 cups) Nestlé Toll House
    semi-sweet chocolate morsels, divided
  3 tablespoons butter
1¼ cups chocolate wafer crumbs

FUDGE SAUCE:
1½ cups Nestlé Toll House semi-sweet chocolate
    morsels, reserved from 12-ounce package
  ½ cup heavy cream
  3 tablespoons butter
  1 tablespoon coffee flavored liqueur

FILLING:
  1 quart coffee ice cream, softened
  2 tablespoons coffee flavored liqueur
    Whipped cream (optional)

Chocolate Cookie Crust: Combine over hot (not boiling) water, ½ cup Nestlé Toll House semi-sweet chocolate morsels and butter; stir until morsels are melted and mixture is smooth. Add chocolate wafer crumbs; stir until well blended. Press into 9-inch pie pan. Chill until firm (35–45 minutes).

Fudge Sauce: Combine over hot (not boiling) water, remaining 1½ cups Nestlé Toll House semi-sweet chocolate morsels, heavy cream and butter. Stir until morsels are melted and mixture is smooth. Remove from heat; stir in coffee flavored liqueur. Chill 10 minutes. Spread ½ cup sauce on bottom of prepared Chocolate Cookie Crust. Chill 15 minutes.

Filling: In large bowl, combine ice cream and coffee flavored liqueur. Spoon over Fudge Sauce layer. Freeze several hours or until firm. Reheat remaining Fudge Sauce over hot (not boiling) water. Serve pie with warm Fudge Sauce and whipped cream.

Classic Mud Pie

Toll House™ Pie

Toll House™ Pie

Makes one 9-inch pie

  2 eggs
  ½ cup all-purpose flour
  ½ cup sugar
  ½ cup firmly packed brown sugar
  1 cup butter, melted and cooled to room
    temperature
One 6-ounce package (1 cup) Nestlé Toll House
    semi-sweet chocolate morsels
  1 cup chopped walnuts
One 9-inch unbaked pie shell*
    Whipped cream or ice cream (optional)

Preheat oven to 325°F. In large bowl, beat eggs until foamy. Add flour, sugar and brown sugar; beat until well blended. Blend in melted butter. Stir in Nestlé Toll House semi-sweet chocolate morsels and walnuts. Pour into pie shell.* Bake at 325°F. for 1 hour. Serve warm with whipped cream or ice cream, if desired.

*If using frozen pie shell, it's necessary to use deep dish style, thawed. Place on cookie sheet and bake additional 10 minutes.

Recipe may be doubled. Bake two pies; freeze one for later use.

Cafe Cream Pie

Makes one 9-inch pie

CHOCO-NUT CRUST:
One 6-ounce package (1 cup) Nestlé Toll House
  semi-sweet chocolate morsels
1 tablespoon vegetable shortening
1½ cups finely chopped nuts

FILLING:
½ pound marshmallows (about 40 large)
⅓ cup milk
¼ teaspoon salt
3 tablespoons coffee flavored liqueur
3 tablespoons vodka
1½ cups heavy cream, whipped   *(continued)*

Choco-Nut Crust: Combine over hot (not boiling) water, Nestlé Toll House semi-sweet chocolate morsels and shortening; stir until morsels are melted and mixture is smooth. Stir in nuts. Spread evenly on bottom and up sides (not over rim) of foil-lined 9-inch pie pan. Chill until firm (about 1 hour). Lift chocolate crust out of pan; peel off foil and place crust back into pie pan or onto serving plate. Chill until ready to use.

Filling: Combine over hot (not boiling) water, marshmallows, milk and salt; stir until marshmallows are melted. Remove from heat. Add coffee flavored liqueur and vodka; stir until well blended. Transfer to medium bowl. Chill until slightly thickened (about 45–60 minutes), stirring occasionally. Gently fold in whipped cream. Pour into prepared Choco-Nut Crust; chill until firm (about 1 hour). Garnish as desired.

Cafe Cream Pie

Best-of-All Black Bottom Pie

Makes one 9-inch pie

GRAHAM CRACKER CRUST:
1¼ cups graham cracker crumbs
6 tablespoons butter, melted
¼ cup sugar

CHOCOLATE LAYER:
⅓ cup sugar
¼ cup cornstarch
¼ teaspoon salt
2 cups milk
3 egg yolks
One 6-ounce package (1 cup) Nestlé Toll House
    semi-sweet chocolate morsels
1 teaspoon vanilla extract

VANILLA LAYER:
¼ cup cold water
1 envelope unflavored gelatin
2 tablespoons rum
3 egg whites
¼ teaspoon cream of tartar
½ cup sugar
    Whipped cream and chocolate shavings
    (optional)

Graham Cracker Crust: In small bowl, combine graham cracker crumbs, butter and sugar. Press evenly on bottom and sides of 9-inch pie plate. Chill until firm (about 1 hour).

Chocolate Layer: In medium saucepan, combine sugar, cornstarch and salt. Gradually stir in milk. Cook over medium heat, stirring constantly, until mixture *boils*. Remove from heat. In small bowl, beat egg yolks. Gradually stir in small amount of hot mixture; return to saucepan. Cook over low heat, stirring constantly, for 2 minutes. Remove from heat. Remove 1½ cups custard to medium bowl; add Nestlé Toll House semi-sweet chocolate morsels and vanilla extract. Stir until morsels are melted and mixture is smooth. Pour into prepared Graham Cracker Crust; chill until set (about 30 minutes). While Chocolate Layer is chilling, prepare Vanilla Layer.

Vanilla Layer: In large bowl, combine cold water and gelatin; let stand 5 minutes. Add remaining warm custard; stir until gelatin dissolves. Cool 15 minutes. Stir in rum; beat with wire whisk until smooth. Set aside. In 1½-quart bowl, combine egg whites and cream of tartar; beat until foamy. Gradually add sugar; beat until stiff peaks form. Fold egg whites into custard; pour over chocolate layer. Chill until set (about 2 hours). Garnish with whipped cream and chocolate shavings, if desired.

Quick Butterscotch Ice Cream Pie

Quick Butterscotch Ice Cream Pie

Makes one 9-inch pie

CRUST:
1½ cups chopped toasted pecans, divided
1 cup graham cracker crumbs
⅓ cup butter, melted

FILLING:
½ cup sugar
½ cup water
½ of 12-ounce package (1 cup) Nestlé Toll House
    butterscotch flavored morsels
2 eggs
½ teaspoon salt
⅛ teaspoon nutmeg
1¾ cups heavy cream, whipped

Crust: In small bowl, combine ½ cup pecans, graham cracker crumbs and butter; mix well. Press crumb mixture into 9-inch pie plate; set aside.

Filling: In small saucepan, combine sugar and water. Bring to *boil* over medium heat; *boil* 3 *minutes*. Remove from heat. In blender container, combine Nestlé Toll House butterscotch flavored morsels and sugar mixture; cover and blend at high speed 30 seconds. Add eggs, salt and nutmeg; cover and blend at high speed 1 minute. Cool to room temperature. Fold into whipped cream. Spoon ½ of Filling into prepared Crust. Sprinkle ½ cup pecans on top. Spoon remaining Filling on top. Garnish with remaining ½ cup pecans. Freeze several hours or until firm.

Butterscotch Rum Chiffon Pie

Makes one 9-inch pie

1 envelope unflavored gelatin
¼ cup cold water
4 eggs, separated
½ cup milk
½ teaspoon salt
½ of 12-ounce package (1 cup) Nestlé Toll House butterscotch flavored morsels
1 tablespoon rum
¼ cup sugar
½ cup heavy cream, whipped
One 9-inch *baked* pie shell*

In cup, combine gelatin and cold water; set aside. Combine over hot (not boiling) water, egg yolks, milk and salt. Cook, stirring constantly with wire whisk, until slightly thickened. Remove from heat. Stir in gelatin until dissolved. Add Nestlé Toll House butterscotch flavored morsels and rum; stir until morsels are melted and mixture is smooth. Transfer to large bowl. Chill, stirring occasionally, until mixture mounds slightly when dropped from spoon (about 20–30 minutes). In 1½-quart bowl, beat egg whites until foamy. Gradually add sugar; beat until stiff peaks form. Fold egg whites and whipped cream into butterscotch mixture. Pour into prepared pie shell.* Chill until firm (about 4 hours).

If using frozen pie shell, it's necessary to use deep dish style.

Frozen Strawberry Fudge Pie

Frozen Strawberry Fudge Pie

Makes one 9-inch pie

Two 10-ounce packages frozen quick thaw strawberries, thawed and drained
¼ cup corn syrup
One 12-ounce container frozen non-dairy whipped topping, thawed, divided
One 9-inch prepared chocolate crumb crust
One 6-ounce package (1 cup) Nestlé Toll House semi-sweet chocolate morsels

Place drained strawberries in blender or food processor container. Cover; process until pureed. Transfer to large bowl. Add corn syrup; mix well. Fold in 2 cups whipped topping. Spoon into crust. Freeze until firm (about 1½ hours). Combine over hot (not boiling) water, 1 cup whipped topping and Nestlé Toll House semi-sweet chocolate morsels; stir until morsels are melted and mixture is smooth. Spread evenly over strawberry layer. Freeze until firm (about 1½ hours). Garnish with remaining whipped topping and chocolate-dipped strawberries, if desired.

Mocha Cheese Pie

Makes one 9-inch pie

One 6-ounce package (1 cup) Nestlé Toll House semi-sweet chocolate morsels
1 tablespoon Taster's Choice freeze dried coffee
1 tablespoon boiling water
Two 8-ounce packages cream cheese, softened
⅓ cup sugar
3 eggs
¼ cup heavy cream
One 9-inch unbaked pie shell*
Sweetened whipped cream (optional)

Preheat oven to 350°F. Melt over hot (not boiling) water, Nestlé Toll House semi-sweet chocolate morsels; stir until smooth. Set aside. In cup, dissolve Taster's Choice freeze dried coffee in boiling water. In large bowl, combine cream cheese and sugar; beat until smooth. Add eggs, 1 at a time, beating well after each addition. Add melted morsels and coffee; mix well. Blend in heavy cream. Pour into prepared pie shell.* Bake at 350°F. for 35–40 minutes. Turn oven off. Let stand in oven with door ajar 15 minutes. Remove. Cool completely; chill. Let stand at room temperature 30 minutes before serving. Garnish with sweetened whipped cream, if desired.

If using frozen pie shell, it's necessary to use deep dish style, thawed. Place on cookie sheet and bake additional 10 minutes.

Chocolate Oatmeal Cookie Pie

Chocolate Oatmeal Cookie Pie

Makes one 9-inch pie

½ cup firmly packed brown sugar
½ cup dark corn syrup
2 eggs
1 teaspoon vanilla extract
½ teaspoon cinnamon
One 6-ounce package (1 cup) Nestlé Toll House
    semi-sweet chocolate morsels
1 cup chopped walnuts
½ cup quick oats, uncooked
½ cup raisins
1 tablespoon grated orange rind
One 9-inch unbaked pie shell*

Preheat oven to 350°F. In large bowl, combine brown sugar, corn syrup, eggs, vanilla extract and cinnamon; beat well. Stir in Nestlé Toll House semi-sweet chocolate morsels, nuts, oats, raisins and orange rind. Pour into prepared pie shell.* Bake at 350°F. for 35–40 minutes. Serve warm. Garnish as desired.

If using frozen pie shell, it's necessary to use deep dish style, thawed. Place on cookie sheet and bake additional 10 minutes.

Frozen Mocha Mousse Pie

Makes one 9-inch pie

1 to 1½ teaspoons Taster's Choice freeze dried
    coffee
1 teaspoon boiling water
½ of 11½-ounce package (1 cup) Nestlé Toll
    House milk chocolate morsels
¾ cup heavy cream, divided
2 egg whites
One 9-inch prepared graham cracker crust
    Whipped cream (optional)

In cup, dissolve Taster's Choice freeze dried coffee in boiling water. Combine over hot (not boiling) water, Nestlé Toll House milk chocolate morsels, ¼ cup heavy cream and coffee; stir until morsels are melted and mixture is smooth. Transfer to large bowl; cool 10–15 minutes. In 1½-quart bowl, beat egg whites until stiff peaks form. Fold into chocolate mixture. In small bowl, beat remaining ½ cup heavy cream until stiff peaks form; fold into chocolate mixture. Spoon into crust. Freeze until firm (about 4 hours). Garnish with whipped cream, if desired.

Chocolate Macadamia Angel Pie

Makes one 9-inch pie

ANGEL PIE CRUST:
- 4 egg whites
- ¼ teaspoon salt
- ¼ teaspoon cream of tartar
- 1 cup sugar

FILLING:
- ¼ cup sugar
- 3 tablespoons cornstarch
- ½ teaspoon salt
- 1½ cups milk
- One 6-ounce package (1 cup) Nestlé Toll House semi-sweet chocolate morsels
- 1 tablespoon chocolate flavored liqueur
- 1½ cups heavy cream, whipped, divided
- 1 cup chopped macadamia nuts
- Chocolate shavings and whole macadamia nuts (optional) *(continued)*

Angel Pie Crust: Preheat oven to 275°F. In 1½-quart bowl, combine egg whites, salt and cream of tartar; beat until foamy. Gradually beat in sugar until stiff peaks form. Spread meringue on bottom and up sides of buttered 9-inch pie plate. Build meringue up around rim, extending 1 inch higher than edge. Bake at 275°F. for 1 hour. Turn oven off. Let stand in oven with door ajar for 1 hour.

Filling: In medium saucepan, combine sugar, cornstarch and salt. Gradually stir in milk. Cook over medium heat, stirring constantly, until mixture *boils*. Boil 1 *minute*; remove from heat. Add Nestlé Toll House semi-sweet chocolate morsels and chocolate flavored liqueur; stir until morsels are melted and mixture is smooth.* Transfer to large bowl; cool to room temperature. Fold in 2 cups whipped cream and chopped nuts. Spoon into prepared Angel Pie Crust. Chill until ready to serve. Garnish with remaining whipped cream and with chocolate shavings and whole nuts, if desired.

Mixture will be thick.

Chocolate Macadamia Angel Pie

CAKES & FROSTINGS

Chocolate Triple Layer Cake

Makes one 3-layer cake

½ of 11½-ounce package (1 cup) Nestlé Toll House milk chocolate morsels
2¼ cups all-purpose flour, divided
1 teaspoon baking powder
1 teaspoon baking soda
⅛ teaspoon salt
6 tablespoons butter, softened
1¼ cups sugar
2 eggs
1 teaspoon vanilla extract
1⅓ cups buttermilk
½ cup chopped toasted hazelnuts
⅓ cup chopped candied cherries
1 cup heavy cream, whipped
Creamy Milk Chocolate Hazelnut Frosting (see page 54)

Preheat oven to 350°F. Grease and flour three 8-inch round baking pans. Melt over hot (not boiling) water, Nestlé Toll House milk chocolate morsels; stir until smooth. Set aside. In small bowl, combine 1¾ cups flour, baking powder, baking soda and salt; set aside. In large bowl, combine butter, sugar, eggs and vanilla extract; beat until creamy. Gradually add flour mixture alternately with buttermilk. Place 1⅔ cups batter into small bowl. Stir in hazelnuts and cherries. Pour into 1 prepared pan. Stir remaining ½ cup flour into plain batter; mix well. Stir in melted morsels. Pour batter into remaining 2 prepared pans. Bake at 350°F. for 30–35 minutes. Cool 15 minutes; remove from pans. Cool completely on wire racks. Spread ½ whipped cream on one chocolate layer; top with nut/cherry layer. Spread with remaining cream; top with second chocolate layer. Frost with Creamy Milk Chocolate Hazelnut Frosting. Chill before serving.

Mocha Almond Torte

Makes one cake

CAKE:
10 eggs, separated
2½ cups sifted confectioners' sugar
1 tablespoon Taster's Choice freeze dried coffee
2½ cups finely ground almonds

MOCHA FROSTING:
2 teaspoons Taster's Choice freeze dried coffee
2 teaspoons boiling water
One 12-ounce package (2 cups) Nestlé Toll House semi-sweet chocolate morsels
1 cup sweet butter, softened
2 eggs

Cake: Preheat oven to 350°F. Grease 15½×10½×1-inch baking pan; line with waxed paper and grease paper. Set aside. In large bowl, combine egg yolks, confectioners' sugar and Taster's Choice freeze dried coffee; beat until light and fluffy. In large bowl, beat egg whites until stiff peaks form. Gently fold in almonds. Fold egg white mixture into egg yolk mixture. Pour into prepared pan. Bake at 350°F. for 30 minutes. Cake will spring back when touched lightly. Invert cake onto wire rack; remove waxed paper. Cool completely.

Mocha Frosting: In small cup, dissolve Taster's Choice freeze dried coffee in boiling water; set aside. Melt over hot (not boiling) water, Nestlé Toll House semi-sweet chocolate morsels; stir until smooth. Set aside. In medium bowl, combine butter and eggs; beat until creamy. Beat in melted morsels. Add coffee; mix well.

Trim edges of cake. Cut into thirds lengthwise. Fill and frost with Mocha Frosting. Cake should be refrigerated. Let stand at room temperature 15 minutes before serving.

Frosted Chocolate Pumpkin Cake

Cream Cheese Frosting: In small bowl, combine cream cheese, butter and vanilla extract; beat until creamy. Gradually add confectioners' sugar; beat well.

Garnish: In cup, combine 2 tablespoons Nestlé Toll House Little Bits semi-sweet chocolate and nuts.

Frost cake with Cream Cheese Frosting. Sprinkle with Garnish.

Cheesecake Cupcakes

Makes 16 cupcakes

FILLING:
Two 3-ounce packages cream cheese, softened
  ¼ cup sugar
  1 egg
  ⅛ teaspoon salt
One 6-ounce package (1 cup) Nestlé Toll House
    semi-sweet chocolate morsels, divided

CAKE:
  ½ cup Nestlé Toll House semi-sweet chocolate
    morsels, reserved from 6-ounce package
1½ cups all-purpose flour
  1 teaspoon baking soda
  ½ teaspoon salt
  ½ cup sugar
  ⅓ cup vegetable oil
  1 egg
  1 teaspoon vanilla extract
  1 cup water
  Confectioners' sugar

Filling: In medium bowl, combine cream cheese, sugar, egg and salt; beat until creamy. Stir in ½ cup Nestlé Toll House semi-sweet chocolate morsels. Set aside.

Cake: Preheat oven to 350°F. Melt over hot (not boiling) water, remaining ½ cup Nestlé Toll House semi-sweet chocolate morsels; stir until smooth. Remove from heat; set aside. In small bowl, combine flour, baking soda and salt; set aside. In large bowl, combine sugar, vegetable oil, egg and vanilla extract; beat well. Stir in melted morsels. Gradually beat in flour mixture alternately with water. Spoon ½ of batter into 16 paper-lined cupcake pans. Spoon 1 slightly rounded tablespoon Filling over batter. Spoon remaining batter over Filling. Bake at 350°F. for 23–25 minutes. Cool 5 minutes; remove from pans. Cool completely on wire racks. Sprinkle with confectioners' sugar.

Frosted Chocolate Pumpkin Cake

Makes one cake

CAKE:
1¾ cups all-purpose flour
2½ teaspoons baking powder
1¼ teaspoons pumpkin pie spice
  ½ teaspoon baking soda
  ½ teaspoon salt
  1 cup firmly packed brown sugar
  ½ cup butter, softened
  3 eggs
  1 cup solid pack canned pumpkin
  ¾ cup milk
  ½ of 12-ounce package (1 cup) Nestlé Toll House
    Little Bits semi-sweet chocolate

CREAM CHEESE FROSTING:
One 8-ounce package cream cheese, softened
  2 tablespoons butter, softened
  1 teaspoon vanilla extract
  ¾ cup sifted confectioners' sugar

GARNISH:
  2 tablespoons Nestlé Toll House Little Bits semi-
    sweet chocolate
  2 tablespoons finely chopped nuts

Cake: Preheat oven to 350°F. In small bowl, combine flour, baking powder, pumpkin pie spice, baking soda and salt; set aside. In large bowl, combine brown sugar and butter; beat until creamy. Beat in eggs and pumpkin. Gradually beat in flour mixture alternately with milk. Stir in Nestlé Toll House Little Bits semi-sweet chocolate. Pour into greased and floured 13×9-inch baking pan. Bake at 350°F. for 35–40 minutes. Cool completely on wire rack.

(continued)

Cheesecake Cupcakes

Chocolate Almond Marble Pound Cake

Makes one tube cake

⅝ of 12-ounce package (1¼ cups) Nestlé Toll House semi-sweet chocolate morsels, divided
3 cups all-purpose flour
2 teaspoons baking powder
½ teaspoon salt
1½ cups sugar
1 cup vegetable oil
¾ teaspoon almond extract
5 eggs
1 cup milk
Confectioners' sugar (optional)

Preheat oven to 350°F. Melt over hot (not boiling) water, ½ cup Nestlé Toll House semi-sweet chocolate morsels; stir until smooth. Set aside. In medium bowl, combine flour, baking powder and salt; set aside. In large bowl, combine sugar, vegetable oil and almond extract; beat well. Add eggs, 1 at a time, beating well after each addition. Gradually beat in flour mixture alternately with milk. Divide batter in half. Stir melted morsels and remaining ¾ cup Nestlé Toll House semi-sweet chocolate morsels into ½ of batter; mix well. Pour ½ of plain batter into greased and floured 10-inch tube pan. Top with ½ of chocolate batter. Repeat layers with remaining batters. Bake at 350°F. for 65–70 minutes. Cool 15 minutes; remove from pan. Cool completely on wire rack. Sprinkle with confectioners' sugar, if desired.

Chocolate Almond Marble Pound Cake

Cream Sherry Fruit Cake

Makes one fruit cake

One 12-ounce package (2 cups) Nestlé Toll House semi-sweet chocolate morsels
2 cups chopped pitted dates
2 cups chopped pecans
2 cups whole candied cherries
1 cup mixed candied fruit
½ cup cream sherry
6 eggs
1 cup sugar
2 teaspoons vanilla extract
3 cups all-purpose flour
2 teaspoons salt

In large bowl, combine Nestlé Toll House semi-sweet chocolate morsels, dates, pecans, candied cherries and candied fruit; add sherry and let stand 1 hour, stirring occasionally. Preheat oven to 325°F. In large bowl, beat eggs until thick and lemon colored (about 5 minutes). Gradually beat in sugar and vanilla extract; set aside. In medium bowl, combine flour and salt. Stir into fruit mixture; mix well. Fold in egg mixture. Spread into greased and floured 9-inch tube pan. Bake at 325°F. for 1 hour. Cool 15 minutes; remove cake from pan. Cool completely on wire rack.

Chocolate Fudge Cake

Makes one 2-layer cake

¾ of 12-ounce package (1½ cups) Nestlé Toll House semi-sweet chocolate morsels
1½ cups all-purpose flour
1 teaspoon baking soda
½ teaspoon salt
½ cup sugar
½ cup butter, softened
2 eggs
1 cup milk
1 tablespoon vinegar
Chocolate Buttercream Frosting (see page 55)

Preheat oven to 350°F. Melt over hot (not boiling) water, Nestlé Toll House semi-sweet chocolate morsels; stir until smooth. Set aside. In small bowl, combine flour, baking soda and salt; set aside. In large bowl, combine sugar and butter; beat until creamy. Add eggs, 1 at a time, beating well after each addition.* Add melted morsels; mix until well blended. In small bowl, combine milk and vinegar; set aside. Gradually beat in flour mixture alternately with milk mixture. Spoon batter into two greased and floured 9-inch round baking pans. Bake at 350°F. for 20–25 minutes. Cool 15 minutes; remove from pans. Cool completely on wire rack. Fill and frost with Chocolate Buttercream Frosting.

Mixture will appear curdled.

Chocolate Mint Layer Cake

Chocolate Mint Layer Cake

Makes one 2-layer cake

⅔ of 10-ounce package (1 cup) Nestlé Toll House
    mint-chocolate morsels
1¼ cups water, divided
2¼ cups all-purpose flour
  1 teaspoon salt
  1 teaspoon baking soda
  ½ teaspoon baking powder
1½ cups firmly packed brown sugar
  ½ cup butter, softened
  3 eggs
    Chocolate Mint Frosting (see page 55)

(continued)

Preheat oven to 375°F. In small saucepan, combine
Nestlé Toll House mint-chocolate morsels and ¼ cup
water. Cook over medium heat, stirring constantly, until
morsels are melted and mixture is smooth. Cool 10
minutes. In medium bowl, combine flour, salt, baking
soda and baking powder; set aside. In large bowl,
combine brown sugar and butter; beat until creamy.
Add eggs, 1 at a time, beating well after each addition.
Blend in chocolate mixture. Gradually beat in flour
mixture alternately with remaining 1 cup water. Pour
into 2 greased and floured 9-inch round baking pans.
Bake at 375°F. for 25–30 minutes. Cool completely on
wire racks. Fill and frost with Chocolate Mint Frosting.
Garnish as desired.

Chocolate Nutmeg Cake Roll

Makes 15 servings

CAKE:
One 12-ounce package (2 cups) Nestlé Toll House
    semi-sweet chocolate morsels, divided
  ½ cup all-purpose flour
  1 teaspoon baking powder
  ¼ teaspoon salt
  4 eggs, separated
  ½ teaspoon vanilla extract
  ½ cup sugar, divided
    Confectioners' sugar

FILLING:
  3 tablespoons cold water
  1 envelope unflavored gelatin
  ⅓ cup boiling water
1¼ cups Nestlé Toll House semi-sweet chocolate
    morsels, reserved from 12-ounce package
  1 tablespoon sugar
  ¼ teaspoon nutmeg
  ½ teaspoon vanilla extract
  ⅔ cup heavy cream
  1 egg yolk
  ½ cup (about 3) ice cubes

GLAZE:
  ¼ cup Nestlé Toll House semi-sweet chocolate
    morsels, reserved from 12-ounce package
  1 tablespoon vegetable shortening

Cake: Preheat oven to 375°F. Melt over hot (not boiling) water, ½ cup Nestlé Toll House semi-sweet chocolate morsels; stir until smooth. Set aside. In small bowl, combine flour, baking powder and salt; set aside. In large bowl, combine egg yolks and vanilla extract; beat until thick and lemon colored (about 5 minutes). Gradually add ¼ cup sugar, beating until sugar dissolves. Gradually add melted morsels, beating until well blended. In large bowl, beat egg whites until soft peaks form. Gradually add remaining ¼ cup sugar, beating until stiff peaks form. Gently fold egg whites into chocolate mixture. Sprinkle flour mixture over egg mixture; fold in gently. Spread batter into greased and floured 15½×10½×1-inch baking pan. Bake at 375°F. for 12–15 minutes. Immediately loosen edges of cake from pan. Invert onto towel sprinkled with confectioners' sugar. Roll up warm cake, jelly roll style, starting from the short side. Cool cake completely, seam side down, on wire rack.

Filling: In blender container, combine cold water and gelatin; let stand 2 minutes. Add boiling water; cover and blend on high speed until gelatin dissolves (about 10 seconds). Add 1¼ cups Nestlé Toll House semi-sweet chocolate morsels, sugar, nutmeg and vanilla extract. Cover; blend on high speed until smooth (about 30 seconds). With blender on low speed, add cream and egg yolk. Add ice cubes; blend
(continued)

until ice melts and mixture thickens (about 40 seconds). Transfer to small bowl. Place in larger bowl filled with ice water until mixture mounds when dropped from spoon (about 15 minutes).

Glaze: Combine over hot (not boiling) water, remaining ¼ cup Nestlé Toll House semi-sweet chocolate morsels and vegetable shortening. Stir until morsels are melted and mixture is smooth.

Unroll cooled cake; spread Filling evenly over cake to within ½ inch from edge. Roll up cake. Drizzle Glaze on top of cake. Chill until ready to serve.

Chocolate Orange Cake

Makes one tube cake

  4 cups all-purpose flour
  2 teaspoons baking soda
  ½ teaspoon salt
  2 cups sugar
1½ cups milk
  1 cup vegetable oil
  4 eggs
  4 teaspoons vinegar
  2 teaspoons vanilla extract
  1 teaspoon grated orange rind
One 12-ounce package (2 cups) Nestlé Toll House
    Little Bits semi-sweet chocolate
  ¼ cup orange juice
  ¼ cup sifted confectioners' sugar

Preheat oven to 325°F. In medium bowl, combine flour, baking soda and salt; set aside. In large bowl, combine sugar, milk, vegetable oil, eggs, vinegar, vanilla extract and orange rind; beat well. Gradually beat in flour mixture. Stir in Nestlé Toll House Little Bits semi-sweet chocolate. Pour into greased and floured 10-inch fluted tube pan. Bake at 325°F. for 65–70 minutes. Cool 10 minutes; remove from pan onto wire rack. To make glaze: In small bowl, combine orange juice and confectioners' sugar; stir until blended. Pierce cake evenly all over with toothpick. Brush cake with glaze. Cool completely.

Chocolate Nutmeg Cake Roll

Toll House™ Cake

Makes one cake

CAKE:
- 1 cup butter, softened
- 1 cup firmly packed brown sugar
- ⅔ cup sugar
- 4 eggs
- 2 teaspoons vanilla extract
- ½ teaspoon salt
- 2 cups all-purpose flour
- One 12-ounce package (2 cups) Nestlé Toll House Little Bits semi-sweet chocolate, divided

FROSTING:
- 1 cup Nestlé Toll House Little Bits semi-sweet chocolate, reserved from 12-ounce package
- ¾ cup butter, softened
- 1½ cups sifted confectioners' sugar
- 2 teaspoons vanilla extract

Cake: Preheat oven to 350°F. Grease bottom of 15½×10½×1-inch baking pan. Line with waxed paper; set aside. In large bowl, combine butter, brown sugar and sugar; beat until creamy. Add eggs, one at a time, beating well after each addition. Add vanilla extract and salt; mix well. Gradually add flour. Stir in 1 cup Nestlé Toll House Little Bits semi-sweet chocolate. Spread batter into prepared pan. Bake at 350°F. for 20–25 minutes. Cool completely.

Frosting: Melt over hot (not boiling) water, 1 cup Nestlé Toll House Little Bits semi-sweet chocolate; stir until smooth. Set aside. In small bowl, combine butter and confectioners' sugar; beat until creamy. Add melted chocolate and vanilla extract; blend until smooth.

Loosen sides of cake. Invert onto lightly floured cloth. Peel off waxed paper. Trim edges of cake; cut cake crosswise into four 3¾×10-inch sections. Spread 3 slightly rounded tablespoonfuls Frosting on one cake layer. Top with second cake layer. Repeat layers of Frosting and cake. Frost entire cake with remaining Frosting.

Chocolate Hazelnut Gâteau

Chocolate Hazelnut Gâteau

Makes one cake

CAKE:
- One 12-ounce package (2 cups) Nestlé Toll House semi-sweet chocolate morsels, divided
- ¾ cup sugar
- ⅔ cup butter, softened
- 3 eggs, separated
- 1 teaspoon vanilla extract
- ½ teaspoon salt
- ¾ cup all-purpose flour
- ¼ cup milk
- ⅔ cup ground toasted hazelnuts

GLAZE:
- 3 tablespoons butter
- 2 tablespoons corn syrup
- 1 tablespoon water
- 1 cup Nestlé Toll House semi-sweet chocolate morsels, reserved from 12-ounce package

Cake: Preheat oven to 350°F. Melt over hot (not boiling) water, 1 cup Nestlé Toll House semi-sweet chocolate morsels; stir until smooth. Set aside. In large bowl, combine sugar and butter; beat until creamy. Beat in melted morsels, egg yolks, vanilla extract and salt. Gradually add flour and milk; beat well. Stir in hazelnuts. In 1½-quart bowl, beat egg whites until stiff peaks form. Fold into chocolate batter. Spread into greased 9-inch round springform pan. Bake at 350°F. for 25–30 minutes. Cool 10 minutes; remove sides of pan. Cool completely.

Glaze: In small saucepan, combine butter, corn syrup and water; cook over low heat, stirring constantly. Bring to *boil*; remove from heat. Add remaining 1 cup Nestlé Toll House semi-sweet chocolate morsels; stir until morsels are melted and mixture is smooth. Cool to room temperature.

Pour Glaze over cake, covering top and sides. Garnish as desired.

Toll House™ Cake

Butterscotch Pineapple Upside Down Cake

Makes one cake

2 cups all-purpose flour
1½ teaspoons baking powder
½ teaspoon salt
One 12-ounce package (2 cups) Nestlé Toll House butterscotch flavored morsels, divided
¾ cup butter, softened, divided
Two 8-ounce cans sliced pineapple, drained, reserving ¾ cup juice
8 maraschino cherries
1 cup sugar
2 eggs

Preheat oven to 350°F. In medium bowl, combine flour, baking powder and salt; set aside. In 10-inch cast iron skillet over low heat, combine 1 cup Nestlé Toll House butterscotch flavored morsels and ¼ cup butter. Stir until morsels are melted and mixture is smooth. Remove from heat. Arrange pineapple and maraschino cherries in skillet. In large bowl, combine sugar, remaining ½ cup butter and eggs; beat until creamy. Gradually beat in flour mixture alternately with reserved ¾ cup pineapple juice. Stir in remaining 1 cup Nestlé Toll House butterscotch flavored morsels. Pour over pineapple. Bake at 350°F. for 35–40 minutes. Immediately invert onto serving plate.

Toll House™ Pound Cake

Makes one tube cake

3 cups all-purpose flour
½ teaspoon salt
¼ teaspoon baking soda
2½ cups sugar
1 cup butter, softened
6 eggs
1⅓ cups sour cream
1 teaspoon vanilla extract
One 12-ounce package (2 cups) Nestlé Toll House semi-sweet chocolate morsels

Preheat oven to 350°F. In medium bowl, combine flour, salt and baking soda; set aside. In large bowl, combine sugar and butter; beat well. Add eggs, 1 at a time, beating well after each addition. Beat in sour cream and vanilla extract. Gradually blend in flour mixture. Stir in Nestlé Toll House semi-sweet chocolate morsels. Pour into greased and floured 10-inch tube pan. Bake at 350°F. for 70–75 minutes. Cool 15 minutes on wire rack; remove from pan. Cool completely on wire rack.

Butterscotch Pineapple Upside Down Cake

Milk Chocolate Chiffon Cake

Milk Chocolate Chiffon Cake

Makes one tube cake

¼ of 11½-ounce package (½ cup) Nestlé Toll
   House milk chocolate morsels
1¾ cups all-purpose flour
1¼ cups sugar, divided
 1 tablespoon baking powder
 1 teaspoon salt
¼ cup + 3 tablespoons vegetable oil
 6 egg yolks
¾ cup water
 1 tablespoon vanilla extract
 8 egg whites
   Chocolate Brandy Creme (see page 55)

(continued)

Preheat oven to 325°F. Melt over hot (not boiling) water, Nestlé Toll House milk chocolate morsels; stir until smooth. Set aside. In large bowl, combine flour, ¾ cup sugar, baking powder and salt; make well in center. Add vegetable oil, egg yolks, water and vanilla extract to well in flour mixture; beat thoroughly. Stir in melted morsels; set aside. In large bowl, beat egg whites until foamy. Gradually add remaining ½ cup sugar, beating until stiff peaks form. Gently fold into chocolate batter. Pour into ungreased 10-inch tube pan. Bake at 325°F. for 55–60 minutes. Immediately invert pan; cool completely. Remove from pan. Split cake crosswise into 2 layers. Fill with ½ cup Chocolate Brandy Creme; frost with remaining 1½ cups Chocolate Brandy Creme. Garnish as desired.

Toll House™ Carrot Cake

Toll House™ Carrot Cake

Makes 2 dozen 2-inch squares

**2 cups all-purpose flour
1 teaspoon baking powder
1 teaspoon baking soda
1 teaspoon cinnamon
1 teaspoon salt
¼ teaspoon nutmeg
1¼ cups sugar
¾ cup vegetable oil
1 teaspoon vanilla extract
3 eggs
1¾ cups shredded carrots
One 8-ounce can juice packed crushed pineapple
1 cup chopped nuts
One 6-ounce package (1 cup) Nestlé Toll House
    semi-sweet chocolate morsels
Confectioners' sugar**

Preheat oven to 350°F. In medium bowl, combine flour, baking powder, baking soda, cinnamon, salt and nutmeg; set aside. In large bowl, combine sugar, vegetable oil, vanilla extract and eggs; beat until well blended. Gradually beat in flour mixture. Stir in carrots, pineapple, nuts and Nestlé Toll House semi-sweet chocolate morsels. Pour into greased and floured 13×9-inch baking pan. Bake at 350°F. for 45–50 minutes. Cool completely on wire rack. Sprinkle with confectioners' sugar. Cut into 2-inch squares.

Chocolate Baum Torte

Makes one cake

CAKE:
 **⅓ of 6-ounce package (⅓ cup) Nestlé Toll House
    semi-sweet chocolate morsels
 ½ cup butter, softened
 ¾ cup sugar, divided
 1 teaspoon vanilla extract
 7 eggs, separated
 ⅔ cup all-purpose flour
 3 tablespoons cornstarch**

GARNISH:
 **⅔ cup sour cream
 3 tablespoons sugar
 ½ teaspoon lemon juice
    Chocolate Sour Cream Frosting (see page 54)
 1½ cups fresh strawberries, washed, hulled and cut
    into halves**

Cake: Preheat broiler. Grease 9-inch springform pan; set aside. Melt over hot (not boiling) water, Nestlé Toll House semi-sweet chocolate morsels; stir until smooth. Cool to room temperature. In small bowl, combine butter, ½ cup sugar and vanilla extract; beat until creamy. Add egg yolks, 1 at a time, beating well after each addition. In cup, combine flour and cornstarch; add to butter/egg mixture. Divide batter in half. Stir melted morsels into ½ of batter. In large bowl, beat egg whites until soft peaks form. Gradually add remaining ¼ cup sugar, beating until stiff peaks form. Divide egg whites equally between plain and chocolate batters; fold in egg whites.* Spread scant ½ cup chocolate batter into bottom of prepared pan (layer will be very thin). Place pan under broiler so that batter is 5 inches from heat. Broil 1–2 minutes or until baked through. Spread scant ½ cup plain batter on top of baked chocolate layer. Broil as before. Repeat, alternating chocolate and plain layers, making 10 layers in all.

Garnish: In cup, combine sour cream, sugar and lemon juice. Spread over top cake layer. Broil 1 minute or until set. Cool 10–15 minutes. Remove sides of pan; cool completely. Frost sides of cooled cake with 1 cup Chocolate Sour Cream Frosting. Arrange strawberries around edge of cake and in center. Using remaining ½ cup frosting, pipe circle around edge of cake. Chill.

*Batter may appear curdled.

Chocolate Baum Torte

Bountiful Butterscotch Cake

Makes one tube cake

One 12-ounce package (2 cups) Nestlé Toll House
    butterscotch flavored morsels
¼ cup water
3 cups all-purpose flour
1 tablespoon baking powder
1 teaspoon salt
½ cup golden raisins
1 cup butter, softened
1 cup sugar
1 teaspoon vanilla extract
4 eggs
1 cup milk
½ cup finely chopped candied cherries
½ cup chopped toasted almonds
    Confectioners' sugar
                                        (continued)

Preheat oven to 350°F. Combine over hot (not boiling) water, Nestlé Toll House butterscotch flavored morsels and water. Stir until morsels are melted and mixture is smooth. Set aside. In medium bowl, combine flour, baking powder, salt and raisins; set aside. In large bowl, combine butter, sugar and vanilla extract; beat until creamy. Add eggs, 1 at a time, beating well after each addition. Gradually beat in flour mixture alternately with milk. Stir in butterscotch mixture, cherries and almonds. Pour into greased and floured 10-inch fluted tube pan. Bake at 350°F. for 1 hour. Cool completely on wire rack; remove from pan. Sprinkle with confectioners' sugar. Garnish as desired.

Bountiful Butterscotch Cake

Brownie Cream Chip Torte

Makes one torte

TORTE:
One 12-ounce package (2 cups) Nestlé Toll House
    Little Bits semi-sweet chocolate, divided
⅔ cup butter
1½ cups all-purpose flour
1 teaspoon baking powder
½ teaspoon salt
4 eggs
1½ cups sugar
1 teaspoon vanilla extract
½ cup chopped walnuts

CREAM CHIP FROSTING:
2 cups heavy cream
¼ cup sifted confectioners' sugar
1 teaspoon vanilla extract
¾ cup Nestlé Toll House Little Bits semi-sweet
    chocolate, reserved from 12-ounce package

GARNISH:
¾ cup Nestlé Toll House Little Bits semi-sweet
    chocolate, reserved from 12-ounce package

Torte: Preheat oven to 350°F. Line bottom and sides of 15½×10½×1-inch baking pan with heavy duty foil; grease foil and set aside. Combine over hot (not boiling) water, ½ cup Nestlé Toll House Little Bits semi-sweet chocolate and butter. Stir until morsels are melted and mixture is smooth. Remove from heat; cool. In small bowl, combine flour, baking powder and salt; set aside. In large bowl, beat eggs and sugar until light and fluffy. Add cooled chocolate mixture; beat until well blended. Gradually blend in flour mixture. Stir in vanilla extract and walnuts. Spread batter into prepared pan. Bake at 350°F. for 18–20 minutes. Loosen edges of cake; cool completely in pan. Invert onto cookie sheet; gently remove foil.

Cream Chip Frosting: In large bowl, combine heavy cream, confectioners' sugar and vanilla extract; beat until stiff. Fold in ¾ cup Nestlé Toll House Little Bits semi-sweet chocolate.

Trim edges of cake; cut cake crosswise into four 3¾×10-inch sections. Spread about ¾ cup Cream Chip Frosting on 1 layer. Top with second layer. Repeat layers of Frosting and cake. Frost entire cake with remaining Frosting.

Garnish: Sprinkle cake with remaining ¾ cup Nestlé Toll House Little Bits semi-sweet chocolate. Chill until ready to serve.

Strawberry Chocolate Shortcake

Strawberry Chocolate Shortcake

Makes 8 shortcakes

One 6-ounce package (1 cup) Nestlé Toll House
    semi-sweet chocolate morsels, divided
½ cup milk
2 cups all-purpose flour
¼ cup + 2 tablespoons sugar, divided
1 tablespoon baking powder
1 teaspoon salt
½ cup butter
2 pints strawberries, washed, hulled and sliced
    Whipped cream

Preheat oven to 450°F. Combine over hot (not boiling) water, ½ cup Nestlé Toll House semi-sweet chocolate morsels and milk. Stir until morsels are melted and mixture is smooth. Set aside. In large bowl, combine flour, 2 tablespoons sugar, baking powder and salt. With pastry blender or 2 knives, cut in butter until mixture resembles coarse crumbs. Add chocolate mixture; stir until blended. Knead in remaining ½ cup Nestlé Toll House semi-sweet chocolate morsels. On floured board, roll dough to ½-inch thickness. Cut dough into 8 pieces with 3-inch round cookie cutter. Place on ungreased cookie sheet. Bake at 450°F. for 8–10 minutes. Cool completely on wire racks.

In medium bowl, toss strawberries with remaining ¼ cup sugar. Before serving, cut each shortcake in half crosswise. Top bottom half with strawberries and whipped cream. Cover with top half, more strawberries and whipped cream.

Midnight Torte

Makes one 4-layer torte

CAKE:
One 6-ounce package (1 cup) Nestlé Toll House
   semi-sweet chocolate morsels
1¼ cups water, divided
2¼ cups all-purpose flour
   1 teaspoon baking soda
   ¾ teaspoon salt
1½ cups sugar
   ¾ cup butter, softened
   1 teaspoon vanilla extract
   3 eggs

CHOCOLATE FILLING:
One 6-ounce package (1 cup) Nestlé Toll House
   semi-sweet chocolate morsels
   3 tablespoons butter
   5 tablespoons milk
   1 teaspoon vanilla extract
   ¼ teaspoon salt
   3 cups sifted confectioners' sugar

CHOCOLATE GLAZE:
   ½ cup heavy cream
One 6-ounce package (1 cup) Nestlé Toll House
   semi-sweet chocolate morsels
   2 teaspoons Nescafé Classic instant coffee
   ½ teaspoon vanilla extract

Cake: Preheat oven to 375°F. Combine over hot (not boiling) water, Nestlé Toll House semi-sweet chocolate morsels and ¼ cup water. Stir until morsels are melted and mixture is smooth. Remove from heat; set aside. In medium bowl, combine flour, baking soda and salt; set aside. In large bowl, combine sugar, butter and vanilla extract; beat until creamy. Add eggs, 1 at a time, beating well after each addition. Blend in chocolate mixture. Gradually blend in flour mixture alternately with remaining 1 cup water. Pour into 2 greased and floured 9-inch round baking pans. Bake at 375°F. for 30–35 minutes. Cool 10 minutes; remove from pans. Cool completely on wire racks.

Chocolate Filling: Combine over hot (not boiling) water, Nestlé Toll House semi-sweet chocolate morsels and butter. Stir until morsels are melted and mixture is smooth. Remove from heat. Add milk, vanilla extract and salt; mix until well blended. Transfer to medium bowl. Gradually add confectioners' sugar; beat until smooth and creamy.   *(continued)*

Chocolate Glaze: In medium heavy gauge saucepan, combine heavy cream, Nestlé Toll House semi-sweet chocolate morsels and Nescafé Classic instant coffee. Cook over low heat, stirring constantly, until morsels are melted and mixture is smooth. Transfer to small bowl. Stir in vanilla extract. Place in larger bowl filled with ice water, stirring occasionally until mixture thickens slightly (about 15–20 minutes).

Split each cake layer in half horizontally. Spread 3 layers with Chocolate Filling; stack. Top with plain layer. Spread Chocolate Glaze on top and sides of torte. Allow glaze to set (about 10 minutes). Garnish as desired.

Butterscotch Fruit Spice Cake

Makes one tube cake

   2 cups all-purpose flour
   1 tablespoon baking powder
   ¾ teaspoon salt
   ½ teaspoon nutmeg
   ¼ teaspoon ginger
   ¼ teaspoon cloves
1¼ cups vegetable oil
   1 cup sugar
   ¼ cup firmly packed brown sugar
   4 eggs
   1 teaspoon rum extract
One 8-ounce can juice packed crushed pineapple,
   drained, reserving ¼ cup juice
   ½ cup finely chopped dried apricots
   ½ of 12-ounce package (1 cup) Nestlé Toll House
   butterscotch flavored morsels
   ½ cup sifted confectioners' sugar

Preheat oven to 350°F. In medium bowl, combine flour, baking powder, salt, nutmeg, ginger and cloves; set aside. In large bowl, combine vegetable oil, sugar, brown sugar, eggs and rum extract; beat until well blended. Gradually beat in flour mixture. Stir in pineapple, apricots and Nestlé Toll House butterscotch flavored morsels. Pour into greased and floured 10-inch fluted tube pan. Bake at 350°F. for 50–60 minutes. Cool 15 minutes; remove from pan. To make glaze: In small bowl, combine reserved ¼ cup pineapple juice and confectioners' sugar; stir until blended. Pierce cake evenly all over with toothpick. Brush cake with glaze. Cool completely on wire rack.

Midnight Torte

Mocha Loaf Cakes

Makes two loaf cakes

½ cup boiling water
1½ tablespoons Taster's Choice freeze dried coffee
2½ cups all-purpose flour
1 tablespoon baking powder
½ teaspoon salt
1½ cups sugar
1 cup butter, softened
4 eggs
½ cup milk
1 teaspoon vanilla extract
One 6-ounce package (1 cup) Nestlé Toll House
    semi-sweet chocolate morsels
    Confectioners' sugar

Preheat oven to 350°F. In cup, combine boiling water and Taster's Choice freeze dried coffee; set aside. In medium bowl, combine flour, baking powder and salt; set aside. In large bowl, combine sugar and butter; beat until creamy. Add eggs, 1 at a time, beating well after each addition. Add coffee, milk and vanilla extract; beat well.* Gradually beat in flour mixture. Stir in Nestlé Toll House semi-sweet chocolate morsels. Pour into 2 greased and floured 8½×4½×2½-inch loaf pans. Bake at 350°F. for 50–55 minutes. Cool 10 minutes; remove from pan. Cool completely on wire rack. Sprinkle with confectioners' sugar.

Mixture will appear curdled.

Butterscotch
Cream Cheese Frosting

Makes about 2⅓ cups frosting

⅓ of 12-ounce package (⅔ cup) Nestlé Toll House
    butterscotch flavored morsels
One 8-ounce package cream cheese, softened
¼ cup butter, softened
2½ cups sifted confectioners' sugar
1 tablespoon lemon juice

Melt over hot (not boiling) water, Nestlé Toll House butterscotch flavored morsels; stir until smooth. Set aside. In large bowl, combine cream cheese and butter; beat until creamy. Gradually add confectioners' sugar and lemon juice; beat well. Blend in melted morsels; chill 15 minutes before frosting cake. Excellent on carrot or applesauce cake; try on cupcakes. Keep frosted cake refrigerated until ready to serve.

Chocolate Sour Cream Frosting

Makes about 1½ cups frosting

⅔ of 6-ounce package (⅔ cup) Nestlé Toll House
    semi-sweet chocolate morsels
3 tablespoons butter
⅓ cup sour cream
¼ teaspoon vanilla extract
2 to 2½ cups sifted confectioners' sugar

Combine over hot (not boiling) water, Nestlé Toll House semi-sweet chocolate morsels and butter. Stir until morsels are melted and mixture is smooth. Transfer to large bowl; cool 10 minutes. Stir in sour cream and vanilla extract. Gradually add confectioners' sugar, beating until frosting is smooth and of spreading consistency. Frosts Chocolate Baum Torte (see page 48) or will frost 12 cupcakes.

Dublin Special Frosting

Makes about 2 cups frosting

½ of 11½-ounce package (1 cup) Nestlé Toll
    House milk chocolate morsels
1½ cups sifted confectioners' sugar
½ cup butter, softened
½ teaspoon salt
2 tablespoons Irish whiskey
1 teaspoon Nescafé Classic instant coffee

Melt over hot (not boiling) water, Nestlé Toll House milk chocolate morsels; stir until smooth. Set aside. In large bowl, combine confectioners' sugar, butter and salt; beat well. In cup, combine whiskey and Nescafé Classic instant coffee; stir until dissolved. Add to sugar mixture along with melted morsels; beat until light and fluffy. Frosts one 9-inch layer cake.

Creamy Milk Chocolate
Hazelnut Frosting

Makes about 2 cups frosting

½ of 11½-ounce package (1 cup) Nestlé Toll
    House milk chocolate morsels
3 tablespoons butter, softened
1 tablespoon hazelnut flavored liqueur
2¼ cups sifted confectioners' sugar
⅓ cup heavy cream

Melt over hot (not boiling) water, Nestlé Toll House milk chocolate morsels; stir until smooth. Set aside; cool 15 minutes. In large bowl, combine butter and hazelnut flavored liqueur; beat well. Blend in melted morsels. Gradually add confectioners' sugar alternately with heavy cream. Frosts Chocolate Triple Layer Cake (see page 37).

Chocolate Brandy Creme

Makes 2 cups creme

½ of 11½-ounce package (1 cup) Nestlé Toll
  House milk chocolate morsels
1¼ cups heavy cream, divided
1 tablespoon brandy

In medium saucepan, combine Nestlé Toll House milk chocolate morsels and ¼ cup heavy cream. Cook over low heat, stirring occasionally, until morsels are melted and mixture is smooth. Transfer to large bowl. Gradually stir in remaining 1 cup heavy cream and brandy. Chill thoroughly (about 1 hour). Beat until stiff peaks form. Fills and frosts Milk Chocolate Chiffon Cake (see page 47).

Whipped Chocolate Cream Frosting

Makes about 2⅓ cups frosting

½ of 6-ounce package (½ cup) Nestlé Toll House
  semi-sweet chocolate morsels
½ cup heavy cream
1½ cups sifted confectioners' sugar
½ cup butter, softened
½ teaspoon vanilla extract

Combine over hot (not boiling) water, Nestlé Toll House semi-sweet chocolate morsels and heavy cream. Stir until morsels are melted and mixture is smooth. Set aside; chill thoroughly. In large bowl, combine confectioners' sugar, butter and vanilla extract; beat well. Gradually add chocolate mixture; beat until stiff. Delicious on chocolate or yellow layer cake; try on cupcakes.

Chocolate Mint Frosting

Makes about 2 cups frosting

⅓ of 10-ounce package (½ cup) Nestlé Toll House
  mint-chocolate morsels
¼ cup butter
1 teaspoon vanilla extract
¼ teaspoon salt
3 cups sifted confectioners' sugar
6 tablespoons milk

Combine over hot (not boiling) water, Nestlé Toll House mint-chocolate morsels and butter. Stir until morsels are melted and mixture is smooth. Stir in vanilla extract and salt. Transfer to large bowl. Gradually beat in confectioners' sugar alternately with milk; beat until smooth.* Fills and frosts Chocolate Mint Layer Cake (see page 41).

If necessary, add more milk until desired consistency is reached.

Butterscotch Orange Frosting

Makes 2⅓ cups frosting

½ of 12-ounce package (1 cup) Nestlé Toll House
  butterscotch flavored morsels
½ cup butter, softened
2 cups sifted confectioners' sugar
¼ cup orange juice
1 tablespoon grated orange rind

Melt over hot (not boiling) water, Nestlé Toll House butterscotch flavored morsels; stir until smooth. Set aside; cool 15 minutes. In large bowl, beat butter until creamy. Gradually beat in confectioners' sugar alternately with orange juice. Stir in orange rind. Blend in melted morsels. Excellent on spice or yellow layer cake.

Milk Chocolate Frosting

Makes 2½ cups frosting

One 11½-ounce package (2 cups) Nestlé Toll House
  milk chocolate morsels
6 tablespoons butter, softened
½ teaspoon salt
2½ cups sifted confectioners' sugar
¼ cup milk
1 teaspoon vanilla extract

Combine over hot (not boiling) water, Nestlé Toll House milk chocolate morsels, butter and salt. Stir until morsels are melted and mixture is smooth. Remove from heat and transfer to large bowl. Gradually beat in confectioners' sugar alternately with milk.* Beat in vanilla extract. Excellent on yellow or chocolate layer cake or cupcakes.

If necessary, add more milk until desired consistency is reached.

Chocolate Buttercream Frosting

Makes 2⅓ cups frosting

One 6-ounce package (1 cup) Nestlé Toll House
  semi-sweet chocolate morsels
½ cup butter, softened
2 cups sifted confectioners' sugar
5 tablespoons milk
½ teaspoon vanilla extract*

Melt over hot (not boiling) water, Nestlé Toll House semi-sweet chocolate morsels; stir until smooth. Set aside; cool 15 minutes. In large bowl, beat butter until creamy. Gradually add confectioners' sugar alternately with milk. Add melted morsels and vanilla extract; beat until smooth. Fills and frosts Chocolate Fudge Cake (see page 40).

½ teaspoon orange extract may be substituted.

BREADS

Chocolate Apple Bread

Makes one loaf

TOPPING:
- 2 teaspoons sugar
- ¼ teaspoon cinnamon
- ¼ cup finely chopped walnuts

BREAD:
- 2 cups all-purpose flour
- ½ teaspoon salt
- ½ teaspoon baking powder
- ½ teaspoon baking soda
- ½ teaspoon cinnamon
- ¼ teaspoon nutmeg
- ½ cup butter, softened
- 1 cup sugar
- 2 eggs
- 1 teaspoon vanilla extract
- 2 tablespoons buttermilk
- 1 cup coarsely chopped apples
- ½ cup chopped walnuts
- One 6-ounce package (1 cup) Nestlé Toll House semi-sweet chocolate morsels

Topping: In small cup, combine sugar, cinnamon and walnuts. Set aside.

Bread: Preheat oven to 350°F. In medium bowl, combine flour, salt, baking powder, baking soda, cinnamon and nutmeg; set aside. In large bowl, combine butter and sugar; beat until creamy. Add eggs and vanilla extract; mix well. Gradually beat in flour mixture alternately with buttermilk. Stir in apples, walnuts and Nestlé Toll House semi-sweet chocolate morsels. Pour into greased 9×5×3-inch loaf pan. Sprinkle with Topping. Bake at 350°F. for 50–60 minutes. Cool 15 minutes; remove from pan. Cool completely on wire rack.

Easy Chocolate Sweet Rolls

Makes about 1½ dozen rolls

- 3 cups all-purpose flour, divided
- 2 packages active dry yeast
- 1 teaspoon salt
- ½ teaspoon cinnamon
- 1¼ cups water
- ⅓ cup sugar
- ⅓ cup butter
- 1 egg
- 2 tablespoons grated orange rind
- ½ cup raisins
- One 6-ounce package (1 cup) Nestlé Toll House semi-sweet chocolate morsels
- ½ cup sifted confectioners' sugar
- 3 teaspoons orange juice

In large bowl, combine 1½ cups flour, yeast, salt and cinnamon. In small saucepan, combine water, sugar and butter. Cook, stirring constantly, until butter is almost melted (115°–120°F.). Add to flour mixture; beat until smooth. Add egg and orange rind; beat well. Stir in remaining 1½ cups flour and raisins. Cover; let rise in warm place until almost doubled in bulk (about 1 hour). Stir down. Let stand 10 minutes. Stir in Nestlé Toll House semi-sweet chocolate morsels. Fill greased muffin cups ⅔ full. Cover; let rise in warm place until almost doubled in bulk (about 30 minutes). Preheat oven to 425°F. Bake at 425°F. for 10–15 minutes. Cool completely. To make glaze: In small bowl, combine confectioners' sugar and orange juice; beat until smooth. Drizzle rolls with glaze.

Chocolate Chip Brioche

Chocolate Chip Brioche

Makes one brioche

1 package active dry yeast
6 tablespoons warm water (105°–115°F.)
2¾ cups all-purpose flour, divided
2 tablespoons sugar
1 teaspoon salt
6 tablespoons butter, softened
6 tablespoons heavy cream
4 egg yolks
½ of 6-ounce package (½ cup) Nestlé Toll House
   semi-sweet chocolate morsels
1 egg, beaten   *(continued)*

In small bowl, dissolve yeast in warm water; set aside for 10 minutes. Add ¾ cup flour; knead until smooth. Cover with plastic wrap; let rise in warm place for 1 hour. In large bowl, combine remaining 2 cups flour, sugar and salt; make well in center. Add butter, heavy cream and egg yolks to well; mix until dough forms a ball. On lightly floured board, knead dough until smooth and elastic (about 5 minutes). Knead in yeast mixture. Knead in Nestlé Toll House semi-sweet chocolate morsels. Reserve ¼ of dough; set aside. Form remaining dough into ball; place in buttered 8-inch glass brioche mold.* Make deep depression in center of dough. Roll remaining ¼ of dough into ball. Press into center of dough in mold. Pat topknot to shape evenly. Cover with cloth; let rise in warm place until doubled in bulk (about 1 hour). Preheat oven to 350°F. Brush bread with beaten egg. Bake at 350°F. for 40–45 minutes. Cover with foil. Bake 15 minutes longer. Remove from mold; cool on wire rack. Serve warm.

*If a metal brioche mold is used, raise oven temperature to 375°F.

Butterscotch Pillows

Divide dough into 4 pieces. On floured board, roll 1 piece of dough into 12×8-inch rectangle. Cut into six 4-inch squares. Spoon 2 teaspoonfuls Filling in center of each square; bring opposite corners to center. Pinch to seal. Place 2 inches apart on greased cookie sheet. Repeat with remaining dough and Filling. Let rise uncovered in warm place for 30 minutes. Preheat oven to 400°F. Bake at 400°F. for 7–9 minutes. In small saucepan, heat apricot jam over low heat, stirring constantly until melted. Brush pillows with melted jam.

Granola Coffee Ring

Makes one coffee ring

FILLING:
  ½ of 12-ounce package (1 cup) Nestlé Toll House butterscotch flavored morsels, divided
  ½ cup chopped nuts
  ½ teaspoon cinnamon

CAKE:
  1 cup granola cereal
  ¾ cup sour cream
1¼ cups all-purpose flour
  ¾ teaspoon baking soda
  ¾ teaspoon baking powder
  ½ teaspoon salt
  ½ cup butter, softened
  ½ cup sugar
  3 eggs
  ½ teaspoon grated orange rind

GLAZE:
  ½ cup Nestlé Toll House butterscotch flavored morsels, reserved from 12-ounce package
  2 tablespoons finely chopped nuts

Filling: In small bowl, combine ½ cup Nestlé Toll House butterscotch flavored morsels, nuts and cinnamon. Set aside.

Cake: Preheat oven to 350°F. In large bowl, combine cereal and sour cream; let stand 15 minutes to soften cereal. In small bowl, combine flour, baking soda, baking powder and salt; set aside. Add butter, sugar, eggs and orange rind to granola/sour cream mixture; beat well. Gradually blend in flour mixture. Spoon ½ of batter into greased and floured 9-inch tube pan. Cover with Filling. Top with remaining batter. Bake at 350°F. for 50 minutes. Cool cake 15 minutes. Remove from pan; cool completely on wire rack.

Glaze: Melt over hot (not boiling) water, remaining ½ cup Nestlé Toll House butterscotch flavored morsels; stir until smooth. Drizzle Glaze over top of cake. Sprinkle with nuts.

Butterscotch Pillows

Makes 2 dozen pillows

BREAD:
  1 package active dry yeast
  ¼ cup warm water (105°–115°F.)
  ⅓ cup butter, softened
  ¼ cup sugar
  1 teaspoon salt
  ½ cup milk, scalded
  2 eggs
  3 cups all-purpose flour, divided

FILLING:
Two 3-ounce packages cream cheese, softened
  1 tablespoon sugar
  1 egg yolk
  ½ teaspoon vanilla extract
  ½ of 12-ounce package (1 cup) Nestlé Toll House butterscotch flavored morsels

  ¼ cup apricot jam

Bread: In cup, combine yeast and water; stir to soften. Set aside. In large bowl, combine butter, sugar and salt. Add scalded milk; stir until butter is melted. Cool to room temperature. Add eggs and 1 cup flour; beat well. Stir in yeast. Gradually stir in remaining 2 cups flour; mix well. Cover bowl with damp cloth; refrigerate dough about 4 hours.

Filling: In small bowl, combine cream cheese, sugar, egg yolk and vanilla extract; beat until creamy. Stir in Nestlé Toll House butterscotch flavored morsels.

(continued)

Granola Coffee Ring

Pumpernickel Bread

Pumpernickel Bread

Makes 3 loaves

One 6-ounce package (1 cup) Nestlé Toll House
    semi-sweet chocolate morsels
2 tablespoons butter
3 packages active dry yeast
1½ cups warm water (105°–115°F.)
½ cup molasses
3 tablespoons caraway seed, divided
1 tablespoon salt
2¾ cups rye flour
2½ cups all-purpose flour, divided
    Cornmeal
1 egg, slightly beaten
1 teaspoon water

Combine over hot (not boiling) water, Nestlé Toll
House semi-sweet chocolate morsels and butter. Stir
until morsels are melted and mixture is smooth. Set
aside. In large bowl, dissolve yeast in warm water. Add
molasses, 2 tablespoons caraway seed, salt, rye flour
and melted morsels; beat well. Stir in all-purpose flour,
1 cup at a time, to make a soft dough. Gradually add
remaining ½ cup flour; mix well. Turn dough onto

(continued)

lightly floured board; cover with bowl. Let rest 10
minutes. Knead dough until smooth and elastic (about
15 minutes). Place dough in greased bowl; turn once.
Cover and let rise in warm place 1 hour. Punch dough
down; cover and let rise in warm place 45 minutes.
Punch dough down; divide into 3 equal parts. Shape
each into a ball and place on greased cookie sheet
that has been sprinkled with cornmeal. Cover; let rise
in warm place until doubled in bulk (about 1 hour).
Preheat oven to 375°F. In cup, combine egg and water;
brush tops of loaves with egg mixture and sprinkle
with remaining 1 tablespoon caraway seed. Bake at
375°F. for 30–35 minutes. Cool on wire racks.

Chocolate Pistachio Bread

Makes one horseshoe-shaped loaf

1 package active dry yeast
½ cup + 1 tablespoon sugar, divided
¼ cup warm water (105°–115°F.)
1 cup warm milk (105°–115°F.)
¼ cup butter, softened
2 teaspoons salt
4 cups all-purpose flour
2 tablespoons butter, melted
1 cup coarsely chopped pistachio nuts
One 6-ounce package (1 cup) Nestlé Toll House
    semi-sweet chocolate morsels
1 egg, beaten
½ cup sifted confectioners' sugar
3 teaspoons lemon juice

In large bowl, combine yeast, 1 tablespoon sugar and
water; let stand 10 minutes. Add milk, ¼ cup butter,
salt and remaining ½ cup sugar; mix well. Stir in flour, 1
cup at a time, to form stiff dough. On lightly floured
board, knead dough until smooth and elastic (about 10
minutes). Form into ball; place in greased bowl and
turn once. Cover with plastic wrap; let rise in warm
place until doubled in bulk (about 1 hour).

Punch dough down and turn out on floured board. Roll
into 18×12-inch rectangle; brush surface with melted
butter. Sprinkle with pistachio nuts and Nestlé Toll
House semi-sweet chocolate morsels. Roll up, jelly roll
style, starting with long side. Shape into horseshoe;
seal ends. Place seam side down on greased cookie
sheet. Cover; let rise in warm place until doubled in
bulk (about 30 minutes). Preheat oven to 375°F. Brush
bread with beaten egg. Bake at 375°F. for 30–35
minutes. Cool slightly. To make glaze: In small bowl,
combine confectioners' sugar and lemon juice; beat
until smooth. Drizzle glaze over bread while still warm.
Cool completely on wire rack.

Apricot Orange Bread

Makes one loaf

2 cups all-purpose flour
1 tablespoon baking powder
½ teaspoon salt
¼ teaspoon baking soda
¾ cup sugar
¼ cup butter, softened
½ cup orange juice
2 tablespoons milk
1 egg
1¼ cups chopped dried apricots
¼ of 12-ounce package (½ cup) Nestlé Toll House Little Bits semi-sweet chocolate
½ cup chopped walnuts

Preheat oven to 350°F. In small bowl, combine flour, baking powder, salt and baking soda; set aside. In large bowl, combine sugar and butter; beat well. Add orange juice, milk and egg; beat well. Gradually blend in flour mixture. Stir in apricots, Nestlé Toll House Little Bits semi-sweet chocolate and nuts. Spread into greased and floured 9×5×3-inch loaf pan. Bake at 350°F. for 50–55 minutes. Cool 10 minutes; remove from pan. Cool completely on wire rack.

Chocolate Macadamia Muffins

Makes about 15 muffins

¾ of 12-ounce package (1½ cups) Nestlé Toll House semi-sweet chocolate morsels
⅓ cup butter
1½ cups all-purpose flour
1 teaspoon baking soda
¼ teaspoon salt
1 cup chopped macadamia nuts
⅔ cup sour cream
¼ cup corn syrup
1 egg

Preheat oven to 375°F. Combine over hot (not boiling) water, Nestlé Toll House semi-sweet chocolate morsels and butter. Stir until morsels are melted and mixture is smooth. Set aside. In large bowl, combine flour, baking soda and salt. Add nuts and stir to coat well. Make well in center of flour mixture. In small bowl, combine melted morsels, sour cream, corn syrup and egg; mix until blended. Add to well in flour mixture; stir until just moistened. Spoon into paper-lined muffin cups, filling each about ¾ full. Bake at 375°F. for 15–18 minutes. Cool 5 minutes; remove from pans. Cool completely on wire racks or serve warm.

Apricot Orange Bread

Chocolate and Cherry Braid

Makes one braided loaf

2¼ to 2¾ cups all-purpose flour, divided
2 packages active dry yeast
⅔ cup milk
¼ cup sugar
2 tablespoons butter
½ teaspoon salt
1 egg
One 6-ounce package (1 cup) Nestlé Toll House
    semi-sweet chocolate morsels
½ cup maraschino cherries, halved
1 egg yolk, beaten
½ cup sifted confectioners' sugar
¼ teaspoon vanilla extract
2 teaspoons milk (about)
    Toasted sliced almonds
    Candied cherries, halved

In large bowl, combine 1 cup flour and yeast. In small saucepan, combine ⅔ cup milk, sugar, butter and salt. Cook over medium heat, stirring constantly, until butter is almost melted (115°–120°F.). Add to flour mixture; beat until smooth. Add egg; mix well. Stir in Nestlé Toll House semi-sweet chocolate morsels, maraschino cherries and as much remaining flour as will mix in with spoon. Turn out onto lightly floured board. Knead in enough remaining flour to make a moderately stiff dough that is smooth and elastic (6–8 minutes). Divide dough into 3 equal pieces. Cover; let rest 10 minutes. Roll each piece into 18-inch rope. Braid loosely, beginning in middle and working toward ends. Press ends to seal and tuck under. Place on greased cookie sheet. Cover; place in refrigerator and let rise overnight. Remove from refrigerator and let stand 1 hour at room temperature. Preheat oven to 350°F. Brush bread with beaten egg yolk. Bake at 350°F. for 30–35 minutes. Cool completely on wire rack. In cup, combine confectioners' sugar, vanilla extract and enough milk to make glaze of drizzling consistency. Drizzle bread with glaze. Decorate with sliced almonds and candied cherries.

Toll House™ Crumbcake

Toll House™ Crumbcake

Makes 2 dozen squares

TOPPING:
1 tablespoon all-purpose flour
½ cup firmly packed brown sugar
2 tablespoons butter, softened
½ cup chopped nuts
One 12-ounce package (2 cups) Nestlé Toll House
    Little Bits semi-sweet chocolate, divided

CAKE:
2 cups all-purpose flour
1 teaspoon baking powder
1 teaspoon baking soda
½ teaspoon salt
½ cup butter, softened
1 cup sugar
1 teaspoon vanilla extract
3 eggs
1 cup sour cream
1½ cups Nestlé Toll House Little Bits semi-sweet
    chocolate, reserved from 12-ounce package

Topping: In small bowl, combine flour, brown sugar and butter; mix well. Stir in nuts and ½ cup Nestlé Toll House Little Bits semi-sweet chocolate; set aside.

Cake: Preheat oven to 350°F. In small bowl, combine flour, baking powder, baking soda and salt; set aside. In large bowl, combine butter, sugar and vanilla extract; beat until creamy. Add eggs, 1 at a time, beating well after each addition. Gradually beat in flour mixture alternately with sour cream. Fold in remaining 1½ cups Nestlé Toll House Little Bits semi-sweet chocolate. Spread into greased 13×9-inch baking pan. Sprinkle Topping evenly over batter. Bake at 350°F. for 45–50 minutes. Cool completely. Cut into 2-inch squares.

Chocolate and Cherry Braid

Chocolate Bubble Biscuits

Oatmeal Butterscotch Tea Biscuits

Makes about 1½ dozen biscuits

1 cup all-purpose flour
1 tablespoon baking powder
¾ teaspoon salt
¼ cup vegetable shortening
1 cup quick oats, uncooked
⅜ of 12-ounce package (¾ cup) Nestlé Toll House butterscotch flavored morsels
⅓ cup raisins
½ cup milk
1 egg
1 tablespoon honey
1 tablespoon sugar
¼ teaspoon cinnamon

Preheat oven to 425°F. In large bowl, combine flour, baking powder and salt. Using pastry blender or 2 knives, cut in vegetable shortening until mixture resembles coarse crumbs. Stir in oats, Nestlé Toll House butterscotch flavored morsels and raisins; set aside. In small bowl, combine milk, egg and honey; mix well. Add to flour mixture, stirring until dry ingredients are just moistened. Drop by rounded tablespoonfuls onto ungreased cookie sheets. In cup, combine sugar and cinnamon; sprinkle scant ¼ teaspoon over each biscuit. Bake at 425°F. for 8–10 minutes. Cool on wire racks.

Chocolate Bubble Biscuits

Makes 16 biscuits

2 cups all-purpose flour
¾ cup sugar, divided
4 teaspoons baking powder
½ teaspoon salt
⅔ cup butter, divided
One 6-ounce package (1 cup) Nestlé Toll House semi-sweet chocolate morsels
⅔ cup milk
1 teaspoon cinnamon

In large bowl, combine flour, ¼ cup sugar, baking powder and salt. Using pastry blender or 2 knives, cut in ⅓ cup butter until mixture resembles coarse crumbs. Stir in Nestlé Toll House semi-sweet chocolate morsels. Add milk; stir until dough holds a shape. On floured board, knead dough *lightly*. Roll dough into 16 balls. Preheat oven to 375°F. In small saucepan, melt remaining ⅓ cup butter. Pour ½ of melted butter in 8-inch square baking pan. In cup, combine remaining ½ cup sugar and cinnamon. Sprinkle ⅓ cinnamon/sugar mixture over butter in baking pan. Place dough balls in single layer in pan. Brush with remaining melted butter. Sprinkle with remaining cinnamon/sugar mixture. Bake at 375°F. for 30 minutes. Cool 10 minutes; remove from pan. Serve warm.

Cranberry Nut Holiday Bread

Makes one loaf

2 cups all-purpose flour
½ cup sugar
1½ teaspoons baking powder
½ teaspoon baking soda
½ teaspoon salt
1 cup milk
⅓ cup butter, melted
2 teaspoons vinegar
1 teaspoon grated orange rind
1 egg
One 6-ounce package (1 cup) Nestlé Toll House semi-sweet chocolate morsels
1 cup chopped cranberries
½ cup chopped walnuts
Confectioners' sugar

Preheat oven to 350°F. In large bowl, combine flour, sugar, baking powder, baking soda and salt. Add milk, butter, vinegar, orange rind and egg; mix well. Stir in Nestlé Toll House semi-sweet chocolate morsels, cranberries and walnuts. Spoon into greased and floured 9×5×3-inch loaf pan. Bake at 350°F. for 55–60 minutes. Cool 10 minutes; remove from pan. Cool completely on wire rack. Sprinkle with confectioners' sugar.

Oatmeal Butterscotch Tea Biscuits

Little Bits™ Irish Soda Bread

Chocolate Banana Bread

Makes one loaf

⅓ cup raisins
3 tablespoons rum
1½ cups all-purpose flour
½ teaspoon baking powder
½ teaspoon baking soda
½ teaspoon salt
½ cup sugar
½ cup mashed banana
¼ cup butter, melted and cooled to room
   temperature
1 egg
2 tablespoons milk
½ of 6-ounce package (½ cup) Nestlé Toll House
   semi-sweet chocolate morsels
¼ cup chopped walnuts

In small bowl, combine raisins and rum. Let stand 15 minutes; drain and reserve liquid. Preheat oven to 350°F. In small bowl, combine flour, baking powder, baking soda and salt; set aside. In large bowl, combine sugar, banana, butter, egg and milk; beat well. Gradually beat in flour mixture. Stir in raisins, Nestlé Toll House semi-sweet chocolate morsels and nuts. Spread into greased and floured 8½×4½×2½-inch loaf pan. Bake at 350°F. for 45–50 minutes. Poke holes in top of bread with toothpick. Brush with reserved liquid. Cool 10 minutes; remove from pan. Cool completely on wire rack.

Little Bits™ Irish Soda Bread

Makes one loaf

4 cups all-purpose flour
¼ cup sugar
3 teaspoons baking powder
1 teaspoon baking soda
1 teaspoon salt
¼ cup butter, softened
1 cup golden raisins
¼ of 12-ounce package (½ cup) Nestlé Toll House
   Little Bits semi-sweet chocolate
1⅓ cups buttermilk
1 egg
1 egg yolk
1 tablespoon water

Preheat oven to 375°F. In large bowl, combine flour, sugar, baking powder, baking soda and salt. Using pastry blender or 2 knives, cut in butter until mixture resembles coarse crumbs. Stir in raisins and Nestlé Toll House Little Bits semi-sweet chocolate. In small bowl, combine buttermilk and egg; beat well. Add to flour mixture; stir until dry ingredients are just moistened. On lightly floured board, knead dough (about 3 minutes). Shape into flattened ball. Place on lightly greased baking sheet. Score top of dough with sharp knife to form an x, about ½ inch deep. In cup, combine egg yolk and water. Brush on top of bread. Bake at 375°F. for 50–60 minutes. Serve warm.

Orange Chip Muffins

Makes 12 muffins

2¼ cups all-purpose flour
2½ teaspoons baking powder
½ teaspoon baking soda
¼ teaspoon salt
½ cup sugar
½ cup milk
1 egg
⅓ cup orange juice
¼ cup butter, melted
1 teaspoon grated orange rind,
¼ of 12-ounce package (½ cup) Nestlé Toll House
   Little Bits semi-sweet chocolate

Preheat oven to 425°F. In large bowl, combine flour, baking powder, baking soda and salt; make well in center. In small bowl, combine sugar, milk, egg, orange juice, butter and orange rind; mix until blended. Add to well in flour mixture; stir until dry ingredients are just moistened. Stir in Nestlé Toll House Little Bits semi-sweet chocolate. Spoon into greased muffin cups, filling each about ¾ full. Bake at 425°F. for 15–17 minutes or until lightly browned. Cool on wire rack.

Chocolate Pumpkin Muffins

Chocolate Pumpkin Muffins

Makes 12 muffins

1 ½ cups all-purpose flour
½ cup sugar
2 teaspoons baking powder
½ teaspoon cinnamon
½ teaspoon salt
1 cup milk
½ cup solid pack canned pumpkin
¼ cup butter, melted
1 egg
One 6-ounce package (1 cup) Nestlé Toll House
     semi-sweet chocolate morsels
¼ cup finely chopped nuts

Preheat oven to 400°F. In large bowl, combine flour, sugar, baking powder, cinnamon and salt; make well in center. In small bowl, combine milk, pumpkin, butter and egg; add to well in flour mixture. Add Nestlé Toll House semi-sweet chocolate morsels; stir until dry ingredients are just moistened. Spoon mixture into greased muffin cups, filling each ¾ full. Sprinkle 1 teaspoon nuts over each muffin. Bake at 400°F. for 18–20 minutes. Cool 5 minutes; remove from pans. Cool completely on wire racks.

Chocolate Filled Kuchen

Chocolate Filled Kuchen

Makes one large kuchen

1 package active dry yeast
¼ cup warm water (105°–115°F.)
¾ cup milk, scalded
⅓ cup butter, softened
¼ cup sugar
1 teaspoon salt
2 eggs
½ teaspoon vanilla extract
3½ cups all-purpose flour
One 6-ounce package (1 cup) Nestlé Toll House
    semi-sweet chocolate morsels
½ cup chopped walnuts
1 egg, beaten   *(continued)*

In small bowl, dissolve yeast in water; set aside. In large bowl, combine scalded milk, butter, sugar and salt; stir until butter melts. Beat in eggs and vanilla extract. Stir in yeast. Gradually add flour, beating well after each addition. Turn dough out onto lightly floured board; knead 8 minutes. Place dough in large greased bowl; turn once. Cover bowl with plastic wrap; let rise in warm place until doubled in bulk (about 1½ hours). Turn dough out onto lightly floured board; knead 1 minute. Roll into 22×14-inch rectangle. Sprinkle Nestlé Toll House semi-sweet chocolate morsels and nuts over dough. Roll up jelly roll style starting with long side; seal seam. Form into ring; seal ends. Place seam side down on cookie sheet. Cut ⅔ way through ring at 1-inch intervals, leaving center intact. Gently twist each section. Cover with plastic wrap; let rise in warm place until doubled in bulk (about 1 hour). Preheat oven to 350°F. Brush bread with beaten egg. Bake at 350°F. for 25–30 minutes. Serve warm or at room temperature. Garnish as desired.

Chocolate Raisin Bread

Makes one loaf

One 12-ounce package (2 cups) Nestlé Toll House
  semi-sweet chocolate morsels, divided
  6 tablespoons butter
  2 cups all-purpose flour
  1 teaspoon baking powder
  1 teaspoon baking soda
  1 teaspoon salt
  1 egg
1½ cups milk
  ½ cup sugar
  1 teaspoon vanilla extract
  1 cup coarsely chopped nuts
  ½ cup raisins

Preheat oven to 350°F. Combine over hot (not boiling)
water, 1 cup Nestlé Toll House semi-sweet chocolate
morsels and butter. Stir until morsels are melted and
mixture is smooth. Set aside. In small bowl, combine
flour, baking powder, baking soda and salt; set aside.
In large bowl, combine egg, milk, sugar and vanilla
extract; mix well. Add melted morsels; mix until well
blended. Gradually stir in flour mixture until dry
ingredients are just moistened. Stir in remaining 1 cup
Nestlé Toll House semi-sweet chocolate morsels, nuts
and raisins. Pour into greased 9×5×3-inch loaf pan.
Bake at 350°F. for 65–70 minutes. Cool 10 minutes;
remove from pan. Cool completely on wire rack.

Chocolate Orange Glazed Doughnuts

Makes about 2 dozen glazed doughnuts

DOUGHNUTS:
One 11½-ounce package (2 cups) Nestlé Toll House
  milk chocolate morsels, divided
3½ cups all-purpose flour
  3 teaspoons baking powder
  ¾ teaspoon salt
  ¾ cup sugar
  2 tablespoons vegetable oil
  2 eggs
  ½ cup milk
  1 teaspoon grated orange rind
  1 quart vegetable oil

GLAZE:
  1 cup Nestlé Toll House milk chocolate morsels,
    reserved from 11½-ounce package
  ¼ cup corn syrup
  1 tablespoon butter
  1 tablespoon heavy cream

Doughnuts: Melt over hot (not boiling) water, 1 cup
Nestlé Toll House milk chocolate morsels; stir until
smooth. Set aside; cool to room temperature. In

(continued)

Chocolate Orange Glazed Doughnuts

medium bowl, combine flour, baking powder and salt;
set aside. In large bowl, combine sugar, 2 tablespoons
vegetable oil, eggs, milk and orange rind; mix well.
Gradually add melted morsels and flour mixture; beat
well. On lightly floured board, roll dough to ⅜-inch
thickness. Cut with 3-inch round cookie cutter. Cut out
centers with ¾-inch round cookie cutter. Reroll
remaining dough and cut out. In large heavy gauge
saucepan, heat 1 quart vegetable oil over medium
heat to 375°F. Fry doughnuts, a few at a time, 1 minute
on each side. Doughnuts will rise to surface when they
should be turned. Remove; place on paper towels to
drain.

Glaze: Combine over hot (not boiling) water,
remaining 1 cup Nestlé Toll House milk chocolate
morsels, corn syrup, butter and heavy cream. Stir until
morsels are melted and mixture is smooth.

Spoon scant 2 teaspoons Glaze over top of each
cooled doughnut.

CANDY

Chocolate Almond Bark

Makes 1 pound

One 11½-ounce package (2 cups) Nestlé Toll House
    milk chocolate morsels
 1 tablespoon vegetable shortening
 ½ cup raisins
 ½ cup chopped toasted almonds, divided

Combine over hot (not boiling) water, Nestlé Toll
House milk chocolate morsels and vegetable
shortening. Stir until morsels are melted and mixture is
smooth. Remove from heat; stir in raisins and ¼ cup
almonds. Spread into waxed-paper-lined 13×9-inch
baking pan.* Sprinkle remaining almonds on top. Chill
until ready to serve (about 30 minutes). Before serving,
break into bite-size pieces.

*Make waxed paper long enough so that candy can be easily
lifted out of the pan.*

Old-Fashioned Almond Crunch

Old-Fashioned Almond Crunch

Makes about 2 pounds

   1 cup butter
1¼ cups sugar
   2 tablespoons corn syrup
   2 tablespoons water
   1 cup slivered almonds, toasted
One 11½-ounce package (2 cups) Nestlé Toll House
    milk chocolate morsels

In heavy gauge saucepan, combine butter, sugar, corn
syrup and water. Cook over medium heat, stirring
constantly, until mixture *boils*. *Boil* to brittle stage (300°F.)
on candy thermometer. Remove from heat. Stir in
almonds. Pour into foil-lined 15½×10½×1-inch pan.
Sprinkle Nestlé Toll House milk chocolate morsels
over brittle. Let stand about 5 minutes until morsels
become shiny and soft. Spread evenly over crunch.
Cool to room temperature; chill 1 hour. Break into bite-
size pieces.

Chocolate Almond Bark

Creamy Chocolate Fudge

Makes about 2½ pounds

One 7-ounce jar marshmallow cream
1½ cups sugar
⅔ cup evaporated milk
¼ cup butter
¼ teaspoon salt
One 11½-ounce package (2 cups) Nestlé Toll House
    milk chocolate morsels
One 6-ounce package Nestlé Toll House semi-sweet
    chocolate morsels
1 cup chopped walnuts
1 teaspoon vanilla extract

In heavy gauge saucepan, combine marshmallow cream, sugar, evaporated milk, butter and salt. Bring to *full rolling boil* over medium heat, stirring constantly. *Boil 5 minutes*, stirring constantly. Remove from heat. Add Nestlé Toll House milk chocolate morsels and Nestlé Toll House semi-sweet chocolate morsels; stir until morsels are melted and mixture is smooth. Stir in walnuts and vanilla extract. Pour into foil-lined 8-inch square pan. Chill until firm (about 2 hours).

Creamy Chocolate Fudge (top)
Ultimate Rocky Road (middle)
Prestige Pecan Drops (bottom)

Prestige Pecan Drops

Makes 3 dozen candies

1 cup firmly packed brown sugar
⅓ cup evaporated milk
2 tablespoons corn syrup
One 6-ounce package (1 cup) Nestlé Toll House
    semi-sweet chocolate morsels
½ cup chopped pecans
1 teaspoon vanilla extract
36 pecan halves

In heavy gauge saucepan, combine brown sugar, evaporated milk and corn syrup. Bring to *boil* over medium heat, stirring constantly. *Boil 2 minutes*, stirring constantly. Remove from heat. Add Nestlé Toll House semi-sweet chocolate morsels, chopped pecans and vanilla extract; stir until morsels are melted and mixture has thickened slightly. Drop by rounded teaspoonfuls onto waxed-paper-lined cookie sheet. Press pecan half on top. Chill until firm (about 30 minutes).

Ultimate Rocky Road

Makes about 5 dozen 1-inch squares

One 11½-ounce package (2 cups) Nestlé Toll House
    milk chocolate morsels
2¼ cups miniature marshmallows
½ cup coarsely chopped nuts
¼ cup sunflower seeds

Melt over hot (not boiling) water, Nestlé Toll House milk chocolate morsels; stir until smooth. Remove from heat. Stir in marshmallows, nuts and sunflower seeds. Spread in foil-lined 8-inch square pan. Chill until firm (about 1 hour). Cut into 1-inch squares.

Chocolate Cherry Almond Drops

Makes about 2½ dozen candies

One 12-ounce package (2 cups) Nestlé Toll House
    semi-sweet chocolate morsels
¾ cup chopped candied red cherries
1 cup chopped toasted almonds

Melt over hot (not boiling) water, Nestlé Toll House semi-sweet chocolate morsels; stir until smooth. Stir in cherries and almonds. Drop by rounded teaspoonfuls onto waxed-paper-lined cookie sheet. Chill until firm (about 30 minutes). Store in airtight container in refrigerator.

Chocolate Date Nut Logs

Chocolate Date Nut Logs

Makes about 1½ dozen logs

CENTERS:
- 1 cup chopped pitted dates
- 1 cup finely chopped walnuts
- 1 cup flaked coconut
- ⅓ cup cream of coconut

COATING:
- ⅝ of 12-ounce package (1¼ cups) Nestlé Toll House semi-sweet chocolate morsels
- 1 tablespoon vegetable shortening
- 2 tablespoons finely chopped walnuts

Centers: In large bowl, combine dates, nuts, coconut and cream of coconut. Knead lightly until well blended. Drop by level tablespoonfuls onto waxed-paper-lined cookie sheets. Shape into logs. Chill until firm (about 30 minutes).

Coating: Combine over hot (not boiling) water, Nestlé Toll House semi-sweet chocolate morsels and vegetable shortening. Stir until morsels are melted and mixture is smooth. Remove from heat but keep over hot water. Dip logs in chocolate; shake off excess. Place on wire racks set over waxed paper. Sprinkle each log with about ⅛ teaspoonful chopped nuts. Chill until set (about 15 minutes). Store in airtight container in refrigerator.

Chocolate Macadamia Caramels

Makes 3 pounds

- 1¼ cups milk
- 1 cup sugar
- 1 cup firmly packed brown sugar
- 1 cup corn syrup
- 1 cup sweetened condensed milk
- ¼ cup heavy cream
- One 6-ounce package (1 cup) Nestlé Toll House semi-sweet chocolate morsels
- 2 tablespoons butter, softened
- 1½ cups coarsely chopped macadamia nuts
- 1 teaspoon vanilla extract

In large heavy gauge saucepan, combine milk, sugar, brown sugar, corn syrup, sweetened condensed milk and heavy cream. Cook over low heat, stirring constantly, until sugars dissolve. Stir in Nestlé Toll House semi-sweet chocolate morsels and butter. Cook over low heat, stirring constantly, until temperature reaches 246°F. on candy thermometer. Remove from heat; stir in nuts and vanilla extract. Pour into foil-lined and buttered 13×9-inch pan. Chill until firm (about 30 minutes). Cut into 1-inch squares. Wrap in plastic wrap. Store at room temperature.

Chocolate Macadamia Caramels

Chocolate Peanut Butter Cups

Makes 2 dozen cups

CHOCOLATE CUPS:
One 11½-ounce package (2 cups) Nestlé Toll House milk chocolate morsels
2 tablespoons vegetable shortening
2 dozen 1-inch paper candy cups

PEANUT BUTTER FILLING:
¾ cup creamy peanut butter
¾ cup sifted confectioners' sugar
1 tablespoon butter, melted

Chocolate Cups: Combine over hot (not boiling) water, Nestlé Toll House milk chocolate morsels and vegetable shortening. Stir until morsels are melted and mixture is smooth. Remove from heat but keep over hot water. Coat inside of 24 candy cups using 1 teaspoon chocolate mixture for each. Place candy cups in palm of hand; rotate gently, using rubber spatula to push chocolate up sides. Chill until firm (15–20 minutes).

Peanut Butter Filling: In small bowl, combine peanut butter, confectioners' sugar and butter; mix until well blended. Using slightly rounded teaspoonfuls, shape Peanut Butter Filling into balls. Place 1 ball in each chilled cup and press lightly with fingers to flatten. Spoon 1 level teaspoonful reserved melted chocolate mixture on top and smooth over to seal. Chill until firm (about 45 minutes). Store in airtight containers in refrigerator.

Chocolate Peanut Butter Cups (top)
Lemon Cups Deluxe (middle)
Mocha Truffles (bottom)

Mocha Truffles

Makes about 3½ dozen truffles

½ cup evaporated milk
¼ cup sugar
One 11½-ounce package (2 cups) Nestlé Toll House milk chocolate morsels
2 tablespoons coffee flavored liqueur
3½ dozen 1-inch paper candy cups

In heavy gauge saucepan, combine evaporated milk and sugar. Bring to *boil* over medium heat, stirring constantly. *Boil 3 minutes*, stirring constantly. Remove from heat. Add Nestlé Toll House milk chocolate morsels and coffee flavored liqueur; stir until morsels are melted and mixture is smooth. Transfer to small bowl; cover. Chill until thickened (about 30 minutes). Place in pastry bag fitted with star tip. Pipe mocha mixture into paper candy cups. Chill until ready to serve. Store in airtight container in refrigerator.

Lemon Cups Deluxe

Makes about 3 dozen candies

CHOCOLATE CUPS:
One 11½-ounce package (2 cups) Nestlé Toll House milk chocolate morsels
2 tablespoons vegetable shortening
3 dozen 1-inch paper candy cups

LEMON FILLING:
Rind of 1 lemon, grated
1⅓ cups sifted confectioners' sugar
1½ tablespoons lemon juice

Chocolate Cups: Combine over hot (not boiling) water, Nestlé Toll House milk chocolate morsels and vegetable shortening. Stir until morsels are melted and mixture is smooth. Remove from heat but keep over hot water. Coat inside of 36 candy cups using a scant teaspoonful of chocolate for each. Place candy cups in palm of hand; rotate gently, using rubber spatula to push chocolate up sides. Chill until firm (15–20 minutes).

Lemon Filling: In small bowl, combine lemon rind and confectioners' sugar. Gradually add lemon juice; mix until smooth. Fill each chocolate cup with ½ teaspoonful of filling. Spoon ½ teaspoonful reserved melted chocolate mixture on top and smooth over to seal. Chill until firm (about 45 minutes). Store in airtight containers in refrigerator.

Minty Mallows (top)
Nutty Chocolate Mint Fudge (middle)
Chocolate Fudge Marzipan Squares (bottom)

Nutty Chocolate Mint Fudge

Makes 1¾ pounds

One 7-ounce jar marshmallow cream
1½ cups sugar
⅔ cup evaporated milk
¼ cup butter
¼ teaspoon salt
One 10-ounce package (1½ cups) Nestlé Toll House mint-chocolate morsels
½ cup chopped nuts
1 teaspoon vanilla extract

In heavy gauge saucepan, combine marshmallow cream, sugar, evaporated milk, butter and salt. Bring to *full rolling boil* over medium heat, stirring constantly. *Boil 5 minutes,* stirring constantly. Remove from heat. Add Nestlé Toll House mint-chocolate morsels; stir until morsels are melted and mixture is smooth. Stir in nuts and vanilla extract. Pour into foil-lined 8-inch square pan. Chill until firm (about 2 hours). Cut into 1-inch squares.

Chocolate Fudge Marzipan Squares

Makes 3 dozen squares

MARZIPAN LAYER:
One 8-ounce can almond paste
⅓ cup sweetened condensed milk

FUDGE LAYER:
⅝ of 12-ounce package (1¼ cups) Nestlé Toll House semi-sweet chocolate morsels, divided
⅔ cup sweetened condensed milk

GARNISH:
¼ cup Nestlé Toll House semi-sweet chocolate morsels, reserved from 12-ounce package
½ teaspoon vegetable shortening
36 whole toasted almonds

Marzipan Layer: In small bowl, mash almond paste into small pieces. Add ⅓ cup sweetened condensed milk; beat well. Chill until mixture is stiff (about 15 minutes). Press marzipan layer into foil-lined 8-inch square pan; set aside.

Fudge Layer: Combine over hot (not boiling) water, 1 cup Nestlé Toll House semi-sweet chocolate morsels and ⅔ cup sweetened condensed milk. Stir until morsels are melted and mixture is smooth. Pour over marzipan layer. Chill thoroughly. Invert on board; remove foil.

Garnish: Combine over hot (not boiling) water, remaining ¼ cup Nestlé Toll House semi-sweet chocolate morsels and vegetable shortening. Stir until morsels are melted and mixture is smooth. Transfer to cup. Dip each almond halfway into melted chocolate. Place on marzipan layer in 6 rows of 6 almonds each. Chill until set (about 1 hour). Cut into 36 squares. Store in airtight container in refrigerator.

Minty Mallows

Makes 1½ pounds

One 14-ounce can sweetened condensed milk
One 10-ounce package (1½ cups) Nestlé Toll House mint-chocolate morsels
2 cups miniature marshmallows
1 cup coarsely chopped nuts

Combine over hot (not boiling) water, sweetened condensed milk and Nestlé Toll House mint-chocolate morsels. Stir until morsels are melted and mixture is smooth. In large bowl, combine marshmallows and nuts. Add chocolate mixture; mix well. Spread into foil-lined 9-inch square pan. Chill until firm (about 20 minutes).

Chocolate Hazelnut Truffle Log

Chocolate-Dipped Fruit

Makes 1 cup melted chocolate

One 11½-ounce package (2 cups) Nestlé Toll House
milk chocolate morsels
¼ cup vegetable shortening
Fresh fruit, rinsed, patted dry
Canned fruit, drained, patted dry

Combine over hot (not boiling) water, Nestlé Toll House milk chocolate morsels and vegetable shortening. Stir until morsels are melted and mixture is smooth. Remove from heat but keep over hot water. (If chocolate begins to set, return to heat. Add 1–2 teaspoons vegetable shortening; stir until smooth.) Dip pieces of fruit into chocolate mixture, shaking off excess. Place on foil-lined cookie sheets. Chill until set (about 10–15 minutes). Gently loosen from foil with metal spatula. Chocolate-Dipped Fruit may be kept at room temperature up to 1 hour. If chocolate becomes sticky, return to refrigerator.

Chocolate-Dipped Fruit

Chocolate Hazelnut Truffle Log

Makes one log

One 6-ounce package (1 cup) Nestlé Toll House
semi-sweet chocolate morsels
¼ cup butter, softened
2 egg yolks
2 tablespoons heavy cream
2 tablespoons hazelnut flavored liqueur
½ cup chopped toasted hazelnuts

Melt over hot (not boiling) water, Nestlé Toll House semi-sweet chocolate morsels; stir until smooth. Remove from heat but keep over hot water. Add butter, egg yolks and heavy cream; beat with wire whisk or fork until smooth. Stir in hazelnut flavored liqueur. Transfer to small bowl. Set bowl over larger bowl filled with ice cubes. Chill, stirring occasionally, until fudgelike in consistency yet smooth and creamy (about 30 minutes). Shape into 8-inch log. Roll in hazelnuts. Wrap in waxed paper; chill until ready to serve.

Chocolate Amaretto Truffles (top)
Chocolate Creme de Mints (bottom)

Chocolate Amaretto Truffles

Makes about 2½ dozen truffles

One 11½-ounce package (2 cups) Nestlé Toll House
   milk chocolate morsels
   ¼ cup sour cream
   2 tablespoons almond flavored liqueur
   ⅔ cup finely chopped toasted almonds

Melt over hot (not boiling) water, Nestlé Toll House milk chocolate morsels; stir until smooth. Remove from heat. Blend in sour cream. Add almond flavored liqueur; mix well. Transfer to small bowl. Chill until firm. Drop by rounded teaspoonfuls onto waxed-paper-lined cookie sheets; shape into balls. Roll in almonds. Chill until firm (about 30 minutes).

Chocolate Creme de Mints

Makes about 3½ dozen candies

One 11½-ounce package (2 cups) Nestlé Toll House
   milk chocolate morsels
   ¼ cup sour cream
   2½ tablespoons mint flavored liqueur

Melt over hot (not boiling) water, Nestlé Toll House milk chocolate morsels; stir until smooth. Remove from heat. Blend in sour cream. Stir in mint flavored liqueur. Transfer to small bowl. Chill until thickened (about 30 minutes). Fill pastry bag fitted with decorative tip; pipe 1-inch candies onto foil-lined cookie sheets. Chill until ready to serve.

Butterscotch Popcorn Crunchies

Makes about 3½ quarts

One 12-ounce package (2 cups) Nestlé Toll House
   butterscotch flavored morsels
   1 cup corn syrup
   ¼ cup butter
   12 cups popped popcorn
One 12-ounce can salted peanuts

Preheat oven to 300°F. In heavy gauge saucepan, combine Nestlé Toll House butterscotch flavored morsels, corn syrup and butter. Cook over medium heat, stirring occasionally, until mixture *boils*. Place popcorn and nuts in large greased roasting pan. Pour butterscotch mixture over popcorn; toss to coat well. Bake at 300°F. for 45 minutes, stirring frequently. Remove from oven; stir every 10 minutes until slightly cooled. Cool completely. Store in airtight container.

Butterscotch Popcorn Crunchies

Butterscotch Fudge

Makes about 2⅓ pounds

1 cup finely chopped walnuts, divided
One 7-ounce jar marshmallow cream
1½ cups sugar
⅔ cup evaporated milk
¼ cup butter
¼ teaspoon salt
One 12-ounce package (2 cups) Nestlé Toll House
   butterscotch flavored morsels
1 teaspoon orange extract
1 teaspoon grated orange rind

Foil-line 8-inch square pan. Spread ½ cup walnuts evenly on bottom of pan; set aside. In heavy gauge saucepan, combine marshmallow cream, sugar, evaporated milk, butter and salt. Bring to *full rolling boil* over medium heat, stirring constantly. *Boil 5 minutes,* stirring constantly. Remove from heat. Add Nestlé Toll House butterscotch flavored morsels; stir until morsels are melted and mixture is smooth. Stir in orange extract and orange rind. Pour into prepared pan. Sprinkle remaining ½ cup walnuts on top. Chill until firm (about 2 hours).

Butterscotch Fudge (top)
Chocolate Chip Eggnog Balls (middle)
Macadamia Orange Fudge (bottom)

Macadamia Orange Fudge

Makes about 2½ pounds

3 cups sugar
¾ cup butter
⅔ cup evaporated milk
One 12-ounce package (2 cups) Nestlé Toll House
   semi-sweet chocolate morsels
One 7-ounce jar marshmallow cream
1 cup macadamia nuts
2 tablespoons orange flavored liqueur

In heavy gauge saucepan, combine sugar, butter and evaporated milk. Bring to *full rolling boil* over medium heat, stirring constantly. *Boil 5 minutes,* stirring constantly. Remove from heat. Add Nestlé Toll House semi-sweet chocolate morsels; stir until morsels are melted and mixture is smooth. Add marshmallow cream, nuts and orange flavored liqueur; beat until well blended. Pour into foil-lined 13×9-inch pan. Chill until firm (about 1–2 hours).

Chocolate Chip Eggnog Balls

Makes about 3⅓ dozen balls

Two 3-ounce packages cream cheese, softened
4 cups sifted confectioners' sugar
1 tablespoon heavy cream
1 teaspoon brandy extract
½ teaspoon salt
¼ teaspoon cinnamon
⅛ teaspoon nutmeg
¼ of 12-ounce package (½ cup) Nestlé Toll House
   Little Bits semi-sweet chocolate
1¼ cups finely chopped pecans

In large bowl, combine cream cheese, confectioners' sugar, heavy cream, brandy extract, salt, cinnamon and nutmeg; beat until creamy. Stir in Nestlé Toll House Little Bits semi-sweet chocolate. Drop by rounded teaspoonfuls onto cookie sheets. Chill 5 minutes. Roll into balls. Coat completely with nuts.

DESSERTS

Mocha Chocolate Chip Cheesecake

Makes one cheesecake

CRUST:
2¼ cups graham cracker crumbs
One 12-ounce package (2 cups) Nestlé Toll House Little Bits semi-sweet chocolate, divided
⅔ cup butter, melted and cooled to room temperature

CAKE:
½ cup milk
4 teaspoons Taster's Choice freeze dried coffee
1 envelope unflavored gelatin
Two 8-ounce packages cream cheese, softened
One 14-ounce can sweetened condensed milk
2 cups heavy cream, whipped
1 cup Nestlé Toll House Little Bits semi-sweet chocolate, reserved from 12-ounce package

Crust: In large bowl, combine graham cracker crumbs, 1 cup Nestlé Toll House Little Bits semi-sweet chocolate and butter; mix well. Pat firmly into 9-inch springform pan, covering bottom and 2½ inches up sides. Set aside.

Cake: In small saucepan, combine milk and Taster's Choice freeze dried coffee; sprinkle gelatin on top. Set aside for 1 minute. Cook over low heat, stirring constantly, until gelatin and coffee dissolve. Set aside. In large bowl, beat cream cheese until creamy. Beat in sweetened condensed milk and gelatin mixture. Fold in whipped cream and remaining 1 cup Nestlé Toll House Little Bits semi-sweet chocolate. Pour into prepared Crust. Chill until firm (about 2 hours). Run knife around edge of cake to separate from pan; remove sides.

Chocolate Almond Frozen Mousse

Makes six ½-cup servings

MOUSSE:
One 6-ounce package (1 cup) Nestlé Toll House semi-sweet chocolate morsels
3 egg yolks
¼ cup coffee flavored liqueur (optional)
⅛ teaspoon salt
1 cup heavy cream, whipped
⅔ cup chopped toasted almonds, divided

TOPPING:
⅔ cup heavy cream
2 tablespoons sifted confectioners' sugar
1 teaspoon vanilla extract

Mousse: Melt over hot (not boiling) water, Nestlé Toll House semi-sweet chocolate morsels; stir until smooth. Transfer to large bowl; cool 10 minutes. Using wire whisk, quickly blend in egg yolks, coffee flavored liqueur and salt. Fold in whipped cream. Pour ½ of mixture into foil-lined 3-cup bowl. Spoon ⅓ cup almonds on top; top with remaining chocolate mixture. Freeze 3 hours or until firm.

Topping: In small bowl, combine heavy cream, confectioners' sugar and vanilla extract; beat until stiff.

Unmold mousse onto serving dish; remove foil. Decorate with Topping and remaining ⅓ cup almonds. Let mousse stand at room temperature 10 minutes before serving.

Frozen Chocolate Mousse Cake

Frozen Chocolate Mousse Cake

Makes 10–12 servings

1 teaspoon butter
1 tablespoon sifted confectioners' sugar
One 3-ounce package ladyfingers
One 6-ounce package (1 cup) Nestlé Toll House
    semi-sweet chocolate morsels
3 tablespoons water
4 eggs, separated
¼ cup sugar
1 cup heavy cream, whipped   *(continued)*

Butter sides and bottom of 8-inch springform pan. Sprinkle with confectioners' sugar; swirl pan to coat evenly. Separate ladyfingers. Line sides of springform pan with ladyfingers, rounded sides against pan. Crumble remaining ladyfingers; press into bottom of pan. Combine over hot (not boiling) water, Nestlé Toll House semi-sweet chocolate morsels and water. Stir until morsels are melted and mixture is smooth. Transfer to large bowl. Add egg yolks, 1 at a time, beating well after each addition. Set aside. In 1½-quart bowl, beat egg whites until soft peaks form. Gradually add sugar; beat until stiff peaks form. Fold egg whites and whipped cream into chocolate mixture. Pour into ladyfinger-lined pan. Freeze until firm (about 4 hours). Garnish as desired.

Butterscotch Nut Sauce

In large saucepan, combine milk, rice, sugar and salt. Cook over medium heat, stirring constantly, until mixture starts to *boil*. Reduce heat; cover and simmer 45 minutes or until rice is tender, stirring occasionally. Add Nestlé Toll House milk chocolate morsels and vanilla extract; stir until morsels are melted. Transfer to large bowl; cover. Chill thoroughly (about 2 hours). Fold in whipped cream. Spoon into dessert dishes. Sprinkle with cinnamon.

Chocolate Filled Cream Puff Ring

Makes 8 servings

CREAM PUFF RING:
- 1 cup water
- ½ cup butter
- 1 cup all-purpose flour
- 4 eggs

FILLING:
- ⅔ of 12-ounce package (1⅓ cups) Nestlé Toll House semi-sweet chocolate morsels, divided
- Two 3-ounce packages cream cheese, softened
- ½ cup sifted confectioners' sugar
- 1 tablespoon raspberry flavored liqueur (optional)
- ½ cup heavy cream, whipped

GLAZE:
- ⅓ cup Nestlé Toll House semi-sweet chocolate morsels, reserved from 12-ounce package
- 1 tablespoon vegetable shortening

Cream Puff Ring: Preheat oven to 400°F. In medium saucepan, combine water and butter. Bring to *boil* over low heat. Gradually add flour, stirring constantly until mixture cleans the sides of pan. Remove from heat. Add eggs, 1 at a time, beating well after each addition. Drop by 2 rounded tablespoonfuls onto ungreased cookie sheet, connecting to form circle. Bake at 400°F. for 35–40 minutes. Cool completely.

Filling: Melt over hot (not boiling) water, 1 cup Nestlé Toll House semi-sweet chocolate morsels; stir until smooth. Set aside. In medium bowl, combine cream cheese, confectioners' sugar and raspberry flavored liqueur; beat until creamy. Gradually add melted morsels; beat well. Fold in whipped cream.

Glaze: Combine over hot (not boiling) water, remaining ⅓ cup Nestlé Toll House semi-sweet chocolate morsels and vegetable shortening. Stir until morsels are melted and mixture is smooth.

Slice cream puffs in half horizontally. Fill with Filling. Cover with top half. Drizzle with Glaze.

Butterscotch Nut Sauce

Makes about 1⅓ cups sauce

- ½ of 12-ounce package (1 cup) Nestlé Toll House butterscotch flavored morsels
- ¼ cup evaporated milk
- 5 teaspoons orange flavored liqueur or orange juice
- 5 tablespoons finely chopped orange sections
- 2 tablespoons chopped nuts

Melt over hot (not boiling) water, Nestlé Toll House butterscotch flavored morsels; stir until smooth. Add evaporated milk and orange flavored liqueur; blend with fork or wire whisk until smooth. Stir in orange sections and nuts. Serve warm over ice cream or cake.

Fudgy Rice Pudding Supreme

Makes nine ½-cup servings

- 6 cups milk
- ¾ cup uncooked white rice
- ¼ cup sugar
- ¼ teaspoon salt
- ½ of 11½-ounce package (1 cup) Nestlé Toll House milk chocolate morsels
- 2 teaspoons vanilla extract
- 1 cup heavy cream, whipped
- ¼ teaspoon cinnamon

(continued)

Chocolate Filled Cream Puff Ring

Chocolate Meringue Cups with Chocolate Sauce

Chocolate Meringue Cups with Chocolate Sauce

Makes 12 meringue cups and 1¼ cups sauce

CHOCOLATE MERINGUE CUPS:
  3 egg whites
  ⅛ teaspoon cream of tartar
  ⅛ teaspoon salt
  1 cup sifted confectioners' sugar
  1 teaspoon vanilla extract
One 12-ounce package (2 cups) Nestlé Toll House
    Little Bits semi-sweet chocolate, divided

CHOCOLATE SAUCE:
  1 cup Nestlé Toll House Little Bits semi-sweet
    chocolate, reserved from 12-ounce package
  ½ cup heavy cream
  2 tablespoons butter
  ¼ cup raspberry flavored liqueur

  Ice cream

Chocolate Meringue Cups: Draw twelve 2-inch circles 1 inch apart on parchment-paper-lined cookie sheet. Set aside. Preheat oven to 300°F. In large bowl, combine egg whites, cream of tartar and salt; beat until soft peaks form. Gradually add confectioners' sugar and vanilla extract; beat until stiff peaks form. Fold in 1 cup Nestlé Toll House Little Bits semi-sweet chocolate. Spoon meringue into 12 circles, making well in center of each. Bake at 300°F. for 25 minutes. Turn oven off; let stand in oven with door ajar 30 minutes.

Chocolate Sauce: Combine over hot (not boiling) water, remaining 1 cup Nestlé Toll House Little Bits semi-sweet chocolate, heavy cream and butter. Stir until morsels are melted and mixture is smooth. Stir in raspberry flavored liqueur. Serve warm or chilled.

Remove Chocolate Meringue Cups from paper. Serve with scoop of ice cream and Chocolate Sauce.

Chocolate Mint Baked Custard

Makes 1 quart

  1½ cups milk, divided
   ⅔ of 10-ounce package (1 cup) Nestlé Toll House
     mint-chocolate morsels
  1 cup sweetened condensed milk
  2 eggs

Preheat oven to 350°F. In small saucepan, combine ½ cup milk and Nestlé Toll House mint-chocolate morsels. Cook over low heat, stirring constantly, until morsels are melted and mixture is smooth. Set aside. In large bowl, combine remaining 1 cup milk, sweetened condensed milk and eggs; beat until well blended. Add chocolate mixture; beat well. Pour into 1-quart casserole. Fill 13×9-inch baking pan with 4 cups water. Place casserole in baking pan. Bake at 350°F. for 50–55 minutes. Serve warm or cool completely.

Chocolate Almond Glaze

Makes 1¼ cups glaze

  ⅔ of 6-ounce package (⅔ cup) Nestlé Toll House
    semi-sweet chocolate morsels
  ⅓ cup heavy cream
  ¼ cup butter
  1 cup sifted confectioners' sugar
  1 teaspoon almond extract
  Chopped toasted almonds (optional)

In small saucepan, combine Nestlé Toll House semi-sweet chocolate morsels, heavy cream and butter. Cook over medium heat, stirring constantly, until morsels are melted and mixture is smooth. Transfer to small bowl; cool 15 minutes. Gradually add confectioners' sugar and almond extract; beat well. Perfect for angel food or sponge cake. Pour over cake while glaze is still warm. Garnish with chopped toasted almonds, if desired. Chill to set glaze.

Butterscotch Cinnamon Glaze

Makes about ½ cup glaze

  ¼ of 12-ounce package (½ cup) Nestlé Toll House
    butterscotch flavored morsels
  2 tablespoons butter
  2 tablespoons heavy cream
  ⅛ teaspoon cinnamon
  Dash of nutmeg

In medium saucepan, combine Nestlé Toll House butterscotch flavored morsels, butter, heavy cream, cinnamon and nutmeg. Cook over medium heat, stirring constantly, until morsels are melted and mixture is smooth. Cool 20 minutes. Excellent on sponge or angel food cake. Drizzle glaze over cake.

Frozen Chocolate Soufflé Cordial

Frozen Chocolate Soufflé Cordial

Makes 12 servings

¾ of 12-ounce package (1½ cups) Nestlé Toll
    House semi-sweet chocolate morsels
2 cups heavy cream, divided
1 cup sifted confectioners' sugar
¼ cup milk
6 eggs, separated
½ cup coffee flavored liqueur
2 tablespoons sugar
2 tablespoons ground toasted almonds

Prepare 2-inch foil collar for 1½-quart soufflé dish. Set aside. Combine over hot (not boiling) water, Nestlé Toll House semi-sweet chocolate morsels, ¼ cup heavy cream, confectioners' sugar and milk. Stir until morsels are melted and mixture is smooth. Remove from heat. In small bowl, beat egg yolks until thick. Stir into chocolate mixture. Return to heat. Cook over low heat, stirring constantly, until mixture thickens slightly (about 8–10 minutes). Remove from heat; stir in coffee flavored liqueur. Transfer to large bowl; chill until mixture thickens slightly. In large bowl, beat remaining 1¾ cups heavy cream until stiff. Set aside. In medium bowl, beat egg whites until foamy; gradually beat in sugar until stiff peaks form. Fold egg whites and whipped cream into chocolate mixture. Pour into prepared dish. Sprinkle with almonds. Freeze 5–6 hours. Remove collar. Allow to stand at room temperature 30 minutes before serving.

Little Bits™ Baked Pancake with Fruit

Makes one pancake

¼ cup butter
4 eggs
1 cup milk
1 cup all-purpose flour
½ of 12-ounce package (1 cup) Nestlé Toll House
    Little Bits semi-sweet chocolate
2 cups fresh fruit
  Confectioners' sugar

Preheat oven to 425°F. In oven, melt butter in 10-inch cast iron skillet. In large bowl, combine eggs, milk and flour; beat until foamy. Pour into hot skillet. Bake at 425°F. for 2 minutes. Remove from oven. Sprinkle Nestlé Toll House Little Bits semi-sweet chocolate over pancake. Return to oven. Bake at 425°F. for 17–19 minutes. Top with fresh fruit and sprinkle with confectioners' sugar. Serve immediately.

Little Bits™ Baked Pancake with Fruit

Milk Chocolate Mallow Fudge Sauce

Makes about 2½ cups sauce

One 11½-ounce package (2 cups) Nestlé Toll House milk chocolate morsels
2 cups miniature marshmallows
⅔ cup evaporated milk
3 tablespoons butter
1 teaspoon vanilla extract

Combine over hot (not boiling) water, Nestlé Toll House milk chocolate morsels, marshmallows, evaporated milk and butter. Stir until morsels and marshmallows are melted and mixture is smooth. Remove from heat; stir in vanilla extract. Serve warm over ice cream. Cover and store in refrigerator.*

Reheat sauce over hot (not boiling) water before using OR microwave on high about 1 minute for each 1 cup sauce.

Mocha Walnut Sauce

Makes 2¼ cups sauce

1 tablespoon Taster's Choice freeze dried coffee
1 tablespoon boiling water
½ cup heavy cream
½ cup sugar
One 6-ounce package (1 cup) Nestlé Toll House semi-sweet chocolate morsels
½ cup butter
2 egg yolks
¾ cup chopped walnuts

In measuring cup, dissolve Taster's Choice freeze dried coffee in boiling water; set aside. In heavy gauge saucepan, combine heavy cream and sugar. Bring *just to boil*, stirring constantly, over medium heat. Add Nestlé Toll House semi-sweet chocolate morsels, butter and coffee; stir until smooth. Remove from heat. In small bowl, beat egg yolks. Gradually stir in 2 tablespoons chocolate mixture; mix well. Return to chocolate mixture in saucepan. Cook over low heat, stirring constantly, for 3 minutes; remove from heat. Stir in walnuts. Serve warm over ice cream. Cover and store in refrigerator.*

Reheat sauce over hot (not boiling) water before using OR microwave on high about 1 minute for each 1 cup sauce.

Butterscotch Orange Crepes

Makes about 15 crepes

BUTTERSCOTCH ORANGE FILLING:
½ of 12-ounce package (1 cup) Nestlé Toll House butterscotch flavored morsels
One 8-ounce package cream cheese, softened
2 teaspoons milk
1 tablespoon orange flavored liqueur

ORANGE SAUCE:
⅓ cup butter
¼ cup sugar
¼ cup orange juice
1 tablespoon orange flavored liqueur

CREPES:
¾ cup all-purpose flour
¾ teaspoon salt
3 eggs
1 cup milk
2 tablespoons butter, melted
1 tablespoon grated orange rind
Melted butter

Butterscotch Orange Filling: Melt over hot (not boiling) water, Nestlé Toll House butterscotch flavored morsels; stir until smooth. Set aside. In small bowl, beat cream cheese until smooth. Gradually add melted morsels and milk; beat until well blended. Stir in orange flavored liqueur. Set aside.

Orange Sauce: In small saucepan, combine butter, sugar and orange juice. Stir over medium heat until butter is melted and sugar is dissolved. Stir in orange flavored liqueur. Set aside.

Crepes: In large bowl, combine flour and salt. Set aside. In medium bowl, combine eggs, milk, 2 tablespoons melted butter and grated orange rind; beat until well blended. Gradually add to flour mixture; beat until smooth. Heat 8-inch crepe pan or skillet over medium heat; brush with melted butter. For each crepe, pour about 2 tablespoons batter into pan; immediately turn and tip pan to coat bottom. Cook 10–15 seconds. Flip crepe; cook additional 5 seconds. Remove from pan; repeat with remaining batter.

Spread 1 slightly rounded tablespoonful Butterscotch Orange Filling over each crepe. Fold into triangles or roll up jelly roll fashion; place on serving platter. Spoon Orange Sauce over crepes.

Milk Chocolate Mallow Fudge Sauce (top)
Mocha Walnut Sauce (bottom)

Chocolate Mint Baked Alaska

Chocolate Mint Baked Alaska

Makes one Baked Alaska

CRUST:
One 10-ounce package (1½ cups) Nestlé Toll House
    mint-chocolate morsels, divided
  3 tablespoons butter
1¼ cups chocolate wafer crumbs

FILLING:
  1 cup Nestlé Toll House mint-chocolate morsels,
    reserved from 10-ounce package
  2 tablespoons corn syrup
  2 tablespoons heavy cream
  3 pints vanilla ice cream, softened

MERINGUE:
  4 egg whites
 ½ teaspoon cream of tartar
 ¾ cup sugar

Crust: Combine over hot (not boiling) water, ½ cup
Nestlé Toll House mint-chocolate morsels and butter.
Stir until morsels are melted and mixture is smooth.
Add chocolate wafer crumbs; stir until well blended.
Press into bottom of 9-inch springform pan; freeze
until firm.

(continued)

Filling: Combine over hot (not boiling) water,
remaining 1 cup Nestlé Toll House mint-chocolate
morsels, corn syrup and heavy cream. Stir until
morsels are melted and mixture is smooth. Cool to
room temperature. In large bowl, whip ice cream until
smooth but not melted. Gradually stir in chocolate
mixture (flecks will appear in ice cream). Spoon into
center of Crust, mounding high in center and leaving
¾-inch edge. Using spatula, smooth to form dome.
Freeze until firm. Remove sides of pan. Preheat oven
to 450°F.

Meringue: In large bowl, combine egg whites and
cream of tartar; beat until soft peaks form. Gradually
add sugar; beat until stiff peaks form.

Spread Meringue over ice cream and crust to cover
completely; swirl to decorate. Bake at 450°F. for 4–6
minutes or until lightly browned. Serve immediately.

Chocolate Fruit Pastry

Makes one pastry

 ½ of 17¼-ounce package (1 sheet) pre-rolled
    frozen puff pastry, thawed
 ⅔ cup jam or preserves
 ½ of 6-ounce package (½ cup) Nestlé Toll House
    semi-sweet chocolate morsels
  1 egg
  1 tablespoon water

On lightly floured board, roll puff pastry into 15×11-
inch rectangle. Cut into two 11×6-inch rectangles and
three 11×1-inch strips. Place 1 rectangle on ungreased
cookie sheet. Moisten edges of puff pastry with water.
Place one 1-inch strip on each long side to form rim.
Cut remaining strip in half; overlap on each short side
to complete rim. In small bowl, combine jam and
Nestlé Toll House semi-sweet chocolate morsels.
Spoon filling down center of pastry, leaving rim clear of
filling. Fold second rectangle in half lengthwise. With
sharp knife, leaving 1½-inch border, cut 1-inch-long
lines, ½ inch apart, down length of pastry. Moisten
edges of folded pastry and filled pastry. Set folded
pastry on top of filled pastry. Unfold top pastry and
press edges together. Score border with crisscross
design. Chill 15 minutes. Preheat oven to 425°F. In cup,
combine egg and water; beat with fork. Brush over
pastry. Bake at 425°F. for 20 minutes. Reduce oven
temperature to 350°F. and bake for 15–20 minutes.
Cool completely on wire rack.

Milk Chocolate Cream Pastries

Makes 18 pastries

PASTRY:
One 17¼-ounce package pre-rolled frozen puff
    pastry, thawed
½ cup sifted confectioners' sugar
4 teaspoons water

FILLING:
  2 tablespoons sugar
  4 teaspoons all-purpose flour
⅛ teaspoon salt
½ cup milk
  1 egg yolk
½ of 11½-ounce package (1 cup) Nestlé Toll
    House milk chocolate morsels
  1 teaspoon brandy (optional)
½ cup heavy cream, whipped

Pastry: Unfold 1 pastry sheet onto lightly floured
board. Chill remaining sheet. Cut sheet into nine 3¼-
inch squares. Fold each square in half diagonally to
form triangle. With sharp knife, cut ½-inch-wide strip
starting at right edge of folded base to within ½ inch
of triangle point (leaving strip attached). Repeat on left
side. Unfold triangle. Bring point of right border strip
to left point inside cut border. Attach points with water.
Repeat with left border. Place on ungreased cookie
sheets. Chill 15 minutes. Repeat cutting and folding
with second pastry sheet. Preheat oven to 425°F. Bake
at 425°F. for 10 minutes. Reduce oven temperature to
350°F. and bake for 5–7 minutes. Remove from cookie
sheets; cool 5 minutes. With sharp knife, cut out
centers of each pastry, leaving bottom intact. To make
glaze: In small bowl, combine confectioners' sugar and
water; stir until dissolved. Brush pastries with glaze.

Filling: In heavy gauge saucepan, combine sugar, flour
and salt. Gradually add milk, stirring constantly, until
smooth. Cook over low heat, stirring constantly, until
mixture comes to *boil*. Remove from heat. Add egg
yolk; cook 1 minute. Remove from heat. Add Nestlé
Toll House milk chocolate morsels and, if desired,
brandy; stir until morsels are melted and mixture is
smooth. Transfer to small bowl. Cover surface with
plastic wrap. Cool to room temperature, stirring
occasionally. Fold in whipped cream. Fill each pastry
with 1 slightly rounded tablespoon Filling. Chill until
ready to serve.

Chocolate Custard Sauce Grand Marnier

Chocolate Custard Sauce Grand Marnier

Makes about 2¼ cups sauce

½ cup sugar
1½ teaspoons cornstarch
⅛ teaspoon salt
1½ cups milk
½ cup heavy cream
One 6-ounce package (1 cup) Nestlé Toll House
    semi-sweet chocolate morsels
  1 egg yolk
  1 tablespoon orange flavored liqueur

In heavy gauge saucepan, combine sugar, cornstarch
and salt. Gradually add milk and heavy cream. Cook
over medium heat, stirring constantly, until mixture
comes to a *boil*; *boil 1 minute*. Remove from heat. Add
Nestlé Toll House semi-sweet chocolate morsels; stir
until morsels are melted and mixture is smooth. In
cup, beat egg yolk; blend in 1 tablespoon chocolate
mixture. Return to mixture in saucepan; mix well. Stir
in orange flavored liqueur. Transfer to small bowl. Cool
completely. Refrigerate until ready to serve. Let stand
20 minutes before serving. Serve over pound or angel
food cake, fresh fruit or poached pears.

Icy Good Chocolate Cups

Chocolate Bavarian Cream

Makes 10–12 servings

One 12-ounce package (2 cups) Nestlé Toll House
  semi-sweet chocolate morsels
½ cup milk
1 envelope unflavored gelatin
1 tablespoon water
2 eggs, separated
2 tablespoons brandy (optional)
⅛ teaspoon salt
¼ cup sugar, divided
2 cups heavy cream, divided

Line 1½-quart bowl with plastic wrap; set aside. In
small heavy gauge saucepan, combine Nestlé Toll
House semi-sweet chocolate morsels and milk. Stir
over low heat until morsels are melted and mixture is
smooth. Remove from heat. In cup, sprinkle gelatin
over water; set aside 5 minutes. In 1½-quart bowl,
beat egg yolks. Stir in ¼ cup chocolate mixture; return
to saucepan. Cook over low heat, stirring constantly,
until slightly thickened. Add softened gelatin; stir until
dissolved. Remove from heat. Stir in brandy. Transfer
to large bowl; cool to room temperature. In 1½-quart
bowl, beat egg whites and salt until foamy. Gradually
add 2 tablespoons sugar; beat until stiff peaks form.
Fold into cooled chocolate mixture. In medium bowl,
beat 1 cup heavy cream until stiff; fold into chocolate
mixture. Pour into prepared bowl. Chill until firm.
Unmold onto serving platter; remove plastic wrap. In
medium bowl, combine remaining 1 cup heavy cream
and remaining 2 tablespoons sugar; beat until stiff. Fill
pastry bag fitted with rosette tip; decorate mold.

Icy Good Chocolate Cups

Makes 12 cups

18 chocolate wafers, crushed
3 tablespoons butter, melted
2 cups miniature marshmallows, divided
⅝ of 11½-ounce package (1¼ cups) Nestlé Toll
  House milk chocolate morsels
½ cup half and half
1 cup heavy cream, whipped
⅓ cup chopped toasted cashews

In small bowl, combine chocolate wafer crumbs and
butter; mix well. Spoon 1 tablespoon crumb mixture
into each of 12 foil-lined muffin cups; press firmly. Set
aside remaining cookie crumbs. In medium saucepan
over low heat, combine 1⅔ cups marshmallows, Nestlé
Toll House milk chocolate morsels and half and half.
Stir until morsels are melted and mixture is smooth.
Remove from heat; cool completely. Fold in whipped
cream, remaining ⅓ cup marshmallows and cashews.
Pour ⅓ cup into each prepared muffin cup. Sprinkle
with remaining cookie crumbs. Freeze until firm (about
1 hour).

Chocolate Bavarian Cream

Chocolate Cherry Cheesecake

Chocolate Cherry Cheesecake

Makes one cheesecake

CRUST:
One 8½-ounce package chocolate wafers, finely
    crushed
 ½ cup butter, melted

FILLING:
One 12-ounce package (2 cups) Nestlé Toll House
    semi-sweet chocolate morsels
1½ cups heavy cream
Two 8-ounce packages cream cheese, softened
  ¾ cup sugar
  4 eggs
  ¾ cup cherry flavored liqueur
  1 teaspoon vanilla extract

TOPPING:
One 1-pound can cherry pie filling   *(continued)*

Crust: In large bowl, combine chocolate wafer crumbs and butter. Pat firmly into 9-inch springform pan, covering bottom and 2½ inches up sides. Chill 30 minutes.

Filling: Preheat oven to 325°F. Combine over hot (not boiling) water, Nestlé Toll House semi-sweet chocolate morsels and heavy cream. Stir until morsels are melted and mixture is smooth. Set aside. In large bowl, combine cream cheese and sugar; beat until creamy. Add eggs, 1 at a time, beating well after each addition. Add chocolate mixture, cherry flavored liqueur and vanilla extract; mix until blended. Pour into prepared Crust. Bake at 325°F. for 1 hour. Turn oven off. Let stand in oven with door ajar 1 hour. Remove; cool completely. Chill 24 hours.

Topping: Spread cherry pie filling over top of cheesecake to within 1 inch of edge. Garnish as desired.

Heavenly Chocolate Cheesecake

Heavenly Chocolate Cheesecake

Makes one cheesecake

CRUST:
 2 cups vanilla wafers, finely crushed
 1 cup ground toasted almonds
 ½ cup butter, melted
 ½ cup sugar

CAKE:
One 11½-ounce package (2 cups) Nestlé Toll House
  milk chocolate morsels
 ½ cup milk
 1 envelope unflavored gelatin
Two 8-ounce packages cream cheese, softened
 ½ cup sour cream
 ½ teaspoon almond extract
 ½ cup heavy cream, whipped   *(continued)*

Crust: In large bowl, combine vanilla wafer crumbs, almonds, butter and sugar; mix well. Pat firmly into 9-inch springform pan, covering bottom and 2 inches up sides; set aside.

Cake: Melt over hot (not boiling) water, Nestlé Toll House milk chocolate morsels; stir until smooth. Set aside. Pour milk into small saucepan; sprinkle gelatin on top. Set aside for 1 minute. Cook over low heat, stirring constantly, until gelatin dissolves. Set aside. In large bowl, combine cream cheese, sour cream and melted morsels; beat until fluffy. Beat in gelatin mixture and almond extract. Fold in whipped cream. Pour into prepared pan. Chill until firm (about 3 hours). Run knife around edge of cake to separate from pan; remove sides. Garnish as desired.

Toll House™ Quick Ice Cream

Makes about 1½ quarts

½ cup + 2 tablespoons firmly packed brown sugar
½ cup butter
3 eggs
2 teaspoons vanilla extract
½ teaspoon salt
2 cups heavy cream
½ of 12-ounce package (1 cup) Nestlé Toll House
    Little Bits semi-sweet chocolate
1 cup chopped toasted walnuts

In small heavy gauge saucepan, combine brown sugar and butter. Bring to *boil* over low heat, stirring occasionally; *boil 1 minute*. Remove from heat. In blender container, combine eggs, vanilla extract and salt; cover and blend at medium speed for 30 seconds. Gradually pour in brown sugar mixture; blend at high speed for 1 minute. Set aside; cool to room temperature. In large bowl, beat heavy cream until stiff. Fold in butter/sugar mixture. Fold in Nestlé Toll House Little Bits semi-sweet chocolate and walnuts. Pour into foil-lined 9×5×3-inch loaf pan. Cover with foil; freeze until firm (several hours or overnight).

Brandy Alexander Gems

Makes 24 gems

GEM CUPS:
    Pastry for one crust 9-inch pie

FILLING:
    ⅓ of 12-ounce package (⅔ cup) Nestlé Toll House
        Little Bits semi-sweet chocolate, divided
    ⅓ cup heavy cream
    ¼ cup sugar
    ⅛ teaspoon salt
    2 egg yolks
    1 tablespoon brandy
    Whipped cream

Gem Cups: Preheat oven to 450°F. Cut pastry into 24 circles using 2½-inch round cookie cutter. Press circle in each cup of gem pans.* Bake at 450°F. for 7–9 minutes. Remove from pans. Cool completely on wire racks.

Filling: In small heavy gauge saucepan, combine ½ cup Nestlé Toll House Little Bits semi-sweet chocolate, heavy cream, sugar and salt. Cook over low heat, stirring constantly, until chocolate is melted and mixture is smooth. Remove from heat. In small bowl, beat egg yolks. Stir in ¼ cup chocolate mixture. Return to saucepan; cook 1 minute longer. Stir in brandy. Pour into Gem Cups. Chill. Serve with whipped cream; sprinkle with remaining Nestlé Toll House Little Bits semi-sweet chocolate.

*Gem pans are miniature muffin pans.

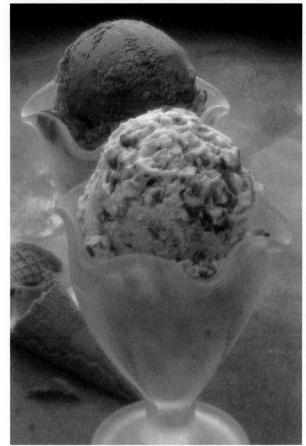

Chocolate Mint Ice Cream (top)
Toll House™ Quick Ice Cream (bottom)

Chocolate Mint Ice Cream

Makes 1 quart

1½ cups heavy cream, divided
1 cup milk
⅓ cup sugar
One 10-ounce package (1½ cups) Nestlé Toll House
    mint-chocolate morsels, divided
2 egg yolks
⅛ teaspoon salt

In heavy gauge saucepan, combine 1¼ cups heavy cream, milk, sugar and 1 cup Nestlé Toll House mint-chocolate morsels. Cook over low heat, stirring with wire whisk, until morsels are melted and mixture is smooth. Remove from heat. In medium bowl, beat egg yolks and salt until thick. Gradually add chocolate mixture; beat until well blended. Chill 30 minutes. In small heavy gauge saucepan, combine remaining ½ cup Nestlé Toll House mint-chocolate morsels and ¼ cup heavy cream. Cook over low heat, stirring constantly, until morsels are melted and mixture is smooth. Remove from heat; set aside. Pour chilled chocolate/egg mixture into electric ice cream freezer; churn until thick (about 25 minutes). Pour in reserved chocolate mixture; churn 10 seconds. Remove dasher; cover and store in freezer until ready to serve.

Chocolate Pistachio Cannolis

Chocolate Pistachio Cannolis

Makes 12 cannolis

½ of 11½-ounce package (1 cup) Nestlé Toll
    House milk chocolate morsels
One 15-ounce container ricotta cheese
Two 3-ounce packages cream cheese, softened
  2 tablespoons sifted confectioners' sugar
  2 tablespoons chopped citron
  1 teaspoon vanilla extract
 12 prepared 5-inch cannoli shells
 ⅓ cup finely chopped pistachio nuts

Melt over hot (not boiling) water, Nestlé Toll House
milk chocolate morsels; stir until smooth. Remove from
heat; cool to room temperature. In large bowl, beat
ricotta cheese until smooth. Add cream cheese,
confectioners' sugar, citron and vanilla extract; beat
well. Blend in melted morsels. Spoon into cannoli
shells. Dip ends in nuts. Chill until ready to serve.

Chocolate Raspberry Meringue

Makes 8 servings

MERINGUE LAYERS:
  2 egg whites
  ⅛ teaspoon cream of tartar
  ⅓ cup sugar
  ¾ of 12-ounce package (1½ cups) Nestlé Toll
    House semi-sweet chocolate morsels, divided
  1 cup chopped toasted almonds

CHOCOLATE SPREAD:
  ½ cup Nestlé Toll House semi-sweet chocolate
    morsels, reserved from 12-ounce package
  2 tablespoons corn syrup
  1 tablespoon heavy cream
  1 tablespoon butter

  1 cup heavy cream, whipped
  1 cup fresh raspberries

Meringue Layers: Draw three 8×4-inch rectangles on
parchment-paper-lined cookie sheet. Set aside.
Preheat oven to 325°F. In small bowl, combine egg
whites and cream of tartar. Beat until soft peaks form.
Gradually add sugar, beating until stiff peaks form.
Fold in 1 cup Nestlé Toll House semi-sweet chocolate
morsels and almonds. Spread 1 cup mixture on each
rectangle. Bake at 325°F. for 25–30 minutes. Cool
completely; remove from paper.

Chocolate Spread: Combine over hot (not boiling)
water, ½ cup Nestlé Toll House semi-sweet chocolate
morsels, corn syrup, 1 tablespoon heavy cream and
butter. Stir until morsels are melted and mixture is
smooth. Chill 30 minutes.

Spread ¼ cup Chocolate Spread on 2 Meringue
Layers. Chill until firm. Place 1 chocolate/meringue
layer on serving tray. Top with ⅔ cup whipped cream
and ½ cup raspberries. Repeat layers. Top with
remaining Meringue Layer and whipped cream.

Chocolate Caramel Sauce

Makes about 2¼ cups sauce

One 11½-ounce package (2 cups) Nestlé Toll House
    milk chocolate morsels
 10 caramels
  ¾ cup milk
  2 tablespoons butter

In medium heavy gauge saucepan, combine Nestlé
Toll House milk chocolate morsels, caramels, milk and
butter. Cook over low heat, stirring constantly, until
morsels and caramels are melted and mixture is
smooth. Serve warm over ice cream. Cover and store
in refrigerator.*

**Remaining sauce must be reheated. Reheat over hot (not
boiling) water OR microwave on high about 1 minute for each
1 cup sauce.*

Satiny Fudge Sauce

Makes about 2¾ cups sauce

One 12-ounce package (2 cups) Nestlé Toll House
    semi-sweet chocolate morsels
  ½ cup butter
  2 cups miniature marshmallows
  ¾ cup milk

Combine over hot (not boiling) water, Nestlé Toll
House semi-sweet chocolate morsels and butter. Stir
until morsels are melted and mixture is smooth. Blend
in marshmallows and milk. Cook, stirring constantly,
until marshmallows are melted. Remove from heat;
cool slightly. Serve warm over ice cream, pound cake
or angel food cake. Cover and store in refrigerator.*

**Reheat sauce over hot (not boiling) water before using OR
microwave on high about 1 minute for each 1 cup sauce.*

Miniature Chocolate Soufflés

Makes 6 servings

One 6-ounce package (1 cup) Nestlé Toll House
semi-sweet chocolate morsels
  4 eggs
  1 egg white
  ⅓ cup milk
  ¼ cup sugar
One 8-ounce package cream cheese, cubed
  Whipped cream, ice cream or sifted
  confectioners' sugar

Preheat oven to 375°F. Melt over hot (not boiling) water, Nestlé Toll House semi-sweet chocolate morsels; stir until smooth. Set aside. In blender container or food processor bowl, combine eggs, egg white, milk and sugar. Cover; process until smooth. With blender or processor running, add cream cheese cubes with blender lid slightly ajar or through the processor feed tube; cover and process until smooth. Add melted morsels; cover and blend just until combined. Pour into 6 ungreased 6-ounce soufflé dishes. Bake at 375°F. for 40 minutes. Soufflés are baked when knife inserted in center comes out clean. Top with whipped cream, ice cream or sifted confectioners' sugar. Serve immediately.

Chocolate Swirl Bavarians

Makes 8 Bavarians

  2 envelopes unflavored gelatin
⅓ cup water
1 cup sugar, divided
¼ cup cornstarch
¼ teaspoon salt
  2 cups milk, scalded
  4 eggs, separated
One 12-ounce package (2 cups) Nestlé Toll House
  semi-sweet chocolate morsels, divided
¼ teaspoon almond extract
  1 cup heavy cream, whipped

In small bowl, combine gelatin and water; set aside. In large saucepan, combine ½ cup sugar, cornstarch and salt. Gradually stir in scalded milk. In small bowl, beat egg yolks with fork. Add some of hot milk mixture to egg yolks; mix well. Return to mixture in saucepan. Cook over medium heat, stirring constantly, until mixture thickens (about 5 minutes). Add softened gelatin; stir until gelatin dissolves. Transfer 1¼ cups custard to bowl. Add 1½ cups Nestlé Toll House semi-sweet chocolate morsels; stir until morsels are melted and mixture is smooth. Transfer remaining custard to another bowl; stir in almond extract. Cover surface of both custards with plastic wrap. Cool to room temperature. In 1½-quart bowl, beat egg whites until foamy. Gradually add remaining ½ cup sugar, beating
(continued)

until stiff peaks form. Fold ½ of egg whites and ½ of whipped cream into chocolate custard. Fold remaining egg whites and whipped cream into almond custard. Divide almond mixture among eight 6-ounce dessert molds. Spoon chocolate custard into pastry bag fitted with wide tip. Insert tip into center of almond mixture. Pipe chocolate mixture into almond mixture until level reaches top of mold. Chill several hours until firm. To unmold: Loosen edge of mold with metal spatula. Set mold in pan of hot water for 10 seconds. Place serving plate over mold and invert. Melt over hot (not boiling) water, remaining ½ cup Nestlé Toll House semi-sweet chocolate morsels; stir until smooth. Drizzle melted morsels over each serving.

Chocolate Fondue Fantasia

Makes about 3 cups fondue

One 12-ounce package (2 cups) Nestlé Toll House
  semi-sweet chocolate morsels
One 14-ounce can sweetened condensed milk
  1 cup milk
  ¼ cup butter
  1 teaspoon vanilla extract
  Fresh fruit
  Pound cake cubes

Combine Nestlé Toll House semi-sweet chocolate morsels, sweetened condensed milk, milk, butter and vanilla extract in electric fondue pot or medium saucepan. Stir over medium heat until morsels are melted and mixture is smooth. Serve with fruit and pound cake cubes for dipping.

Chocolate Fondue Fantasia

INDEX

A

Angel Pie Crust, 36
Anise Cookie Cordials, 23
Apricot Orange Bread, 61

B

Bar Cookies
Black & White Cheesecake
  Brownies, 11
Butterscotch Apricot Streusel
  Bars, 5
Cappuccino Brownies, 20
Cheese Crunchers, 8
Chocolate Macaroon Squares, 20
Chocolate Raspberry Coconut
  Squares, 12
Irish Coffee Brownies, 25
Magic Cookie Bars, 12
Maple Walnut Bars, 12
Milk Chocolate Pecan Bars, 5
Minty Fudge Brownies, 11
No-Bake Butterscotch Snack Bars,
  16
No-Bake Fudge Brownies, 19
Oatmeal Extravaganzas, 27
Spice Islands Butterscotch Bars,
  19
Bavarian Creams
Chocolate Bavarian Cream, 88
Chocolate Swirl Bavarians, 93
Best-of-All Black Bottom Pie, 33
Biscuits and Rolls
Butterscotch Pillows, 58
Chocolate Bubble Biscuits, 64
Easy Chocolate Sweet Rolls, 56
Oatmeal Butterscotch Tea
  Biscuits, 64
Black & White Cheesecake
  Brownies, 11
Bountiful Butterscotch Cake, 50
Brandy Alexander Gems, 91
Breads
Apricot Orange Bread, 61
Butterscotch Pillows, 58
Chocolate and Cherry Braid, 63
Chocolate Apple Bread, 56
Chocolate Banana Bread, 66
Chocolate Bubble Biscuits, 64
Chocolate Chip Brioche, 57
Chocolate Filled Kuchen, 68
Chocolate Macadamia Muffins, 61
Chocolate Orange Glazed
  Doughnuts, 69
Chocolate Pistachio Bread, 60
Chocolate Pumpkin Muffins, 67
Chocolate Raisin Bread, 69
Cranberry Nut Holiday Bread, 64
Easy Chocolate Sweet Rolls, 56
Granola Coffee Ring, 58
Little Bits™ Irish Soda Bread, 66
Oatmeal Butterscotch Tea
  Biscuits, 64

Orange Chip Muffins, 66
Pumpernickel Bread, 60
Toll House™ Crumbcake, 63
Brownie Cream Chip Torte, 51
Brownies
Black & White Cheesecake
  Brownies, 11
Cappuccino Brownies, 20
Irish Coffee Brownies, 25
Minty Fudge Brownies, 11
No-Bake Fudge Brownies, 19
Butterscotch Apricot Streusel Bars, 5
Butterscotch Cinnamon Glaze, 82
Butterscotch Cream Cheese
  Frosting, 54
Butterscotch Crumb Apple Pie, 30
Butterscotch Date Surprise, 6
Butterscotch Fruit Spice Cake, 53
Butterscotch Fudge, 77
Butterscotch Granola Cookies, 13
Butterscotch Lemon Cookies, 14
Butterscotch Nut Sauce, 80
Butterscotch Orange Crepes, 85
Butterscotch Orange Frosting, 55
Butterscotch Pillows, 58
Butterscotch Pineapple Upside
  Down Cake, 46
Butterscotch Popcorn Crunchies, 76
Butterscotch Rum Chiffon Pie, 34

C

Cafe Cream Pie, 32
Cakes
Bountiful Butterscotch Cake, 50
Brownie Cream Chip Torte, 51
Butterscotch Fruit Spice Cake, 53
Butterscotch Pineapple Upside
  Down Cake, 46
Cheesecake Cupcakes, 38
Chocolate Almond Marble Pound
  Cake, 40
Chocolate Baum Torte, 48
Chocolate Cherry Cheesecake, 89
Chocolate Fudge Cake, 40
Chocolate Hazelnut Gâteau, 45
Chocolate Mint Layer Cake, 41
Chocolate Nutmeg Cake Roll, 42
Chocolate Orange Cake, 42
Chocolate Triple Layer Cake, 37
Cream Sherry Fruit Cake, 40
Frosted Chocolate Pumpkin Cake,
  38
Heavenly Chocolate Cheesecake,
  90
Midnight Torte, 53
Milk Chocolate Chiffon Cake, 47
Mocha Almond Torte, 37
Mocha Chocolate Chip
  Cheesecake, 78
Mocha Loaf Cakes, 54
Strawberry Chocolate Shortcake,
  51
Toll House™ Cake, 45
Toll House™ Carrot Cake, 48
Toll House™ Pound Cake, 46
Candy
Butterscotch Fudge, 77

Butterscotch Popcorn Crunchies,
  76
Chocolate Almond Bark, 70
Chocolate Amaretto Truffles, 76
Chocolate Cherry Almond Drops,
  71
Chocolate Chip Eggnog Balls, 77
Chocolate Creme de Mints, 76
Chocolate Date Nut Logs, 72
Chocolate-Dipped Fruit, 75
Chocolate Fudge Marzipan
  Squares, 74
Chocolate Hazelnut Truffle Log, 75
Chocolate Macadamia Caramels, 72
Chocolate Peanut Butter Cups, 73
Creamy Chocolate Fudge, 71
Lemon Cups Deluxe, 73
Macadamia Orange Fudge, 77
Minty Mallows, 74
Mocha Truffles, 73
Nutty Chocolate Mint Fudge, 74
Old-Fashioned Almond Crunch, 70
Prestige Pecan Drops, 71
Ultimate Rocky Road, 71
Cappuccino Brownies, 20
Cheesecake Cupcakes, 38
Cheesecakes
Chocolate Cherry Cheesecake, 89
Heavenly Chocolate Cheesecake,
  90
Mocha Chocolate Chip
  Cheesecake, 78
Cheese Crunchers, 8
Chocolate Almond Bark, 70
Chocolate Almond Frozen Mousse,
  78
Chocolate Almond Glaze, 82
Chocolate Almond Macaroons, 27
Chocolate Almond Marble Pound
  Cake, 40
Chocolate Amaretto Truffles, 76
Chocolate and Cherry Braid, 63
Chocolate Apple Bread, 56
Chocolate Banana Bread, 66
Chocolate Baum Torte, 48
Chocolate Bavarian Cream, 88
Chocolate Brandy Creme, 55
Chocolate Bubble Biscuits, 64
Chocolate Buttercream Frosting, 55
Chocolate Caramel Sauce, 92
Chocolate Cherry Almond Drops, 71
Chocolate Cherry Cheesecake, 89
Chocolate Chip Brioche, 57
Chocolate Chip Eggnog Balls, 77
Chocolate Chip Tarts à l'Orange, 28
Chocolate Cinnabar Wreaths, 16
Chocolate Cookie Crust, 31
Chocolate Cream Strawberry Tart, 29
Chocolate Creme de Mints, 76
Chocolate Custard Sauce Grand
  Marnier, 87
Chocolate Date Envelopes, 27
Chocolate Date Nut Logs, 72
Chocolate-Dipped Brandy Snaps, 17
Chocolate-Dipped Fruit, 75
Chocolate-Dipped Sandwich
  Macaroons, 20

Chocolate Filled Cream Puff Ring, 80
Chocolate Filled Kuchen, 68
Chocolate Fondue Fantasia, 93
Chocolate Fruit Pastry, 86
Chocolate Fudge Cake, 40
Chocolate Fudge Marzipan Squares, 74
Chocolate Glaze, 53
Chocolate Hazelnut Gâteau, 45
Chocolate Hazelnut Truffle Log, 75
Chocolate Macadamia Angel Pie, 36
Chocolate Macadamia Caramels, 72
Chocolate Macadamia Muffins, 61
Chocolate Macaroon Squares, 20
Chocolate Meringue Cups with Chocolate Sauce, 82
Chocolate Mint Baked Alaska, 86
Chocolate Mint Baked Custard, 82
Chocolate Mint Cookies, 22
Chocolate Mint Frosting, 55
Chocolate Mint Ice Cream, 91
Chocolate Mint Layer Cake, 41
Chocolate Mint Meltaways, 23
Chocolate Mint Pinwheels, 11
Chocolate Mint Sugar Cookie Drops, 25
Chocolate Nutmeg Cake Roll, 42
Chocolate Oatmeal Cookie Pie, 35
Chocolate Orange Cake, 42
Chocolate Orange Glazed Doughnuts, 69
Chocolate Orange Granola Cookies, 19
Chocolate Peanut Butter Cups, 73
Chocolate Pistachio Bread, 60
Chocolate Pistachio Cannolis, 92
Chocolate Pumpkin Muffins, 67
Chocolate Raisin Bread, 69
Chocolate Raspberry Coconut Squares, 12
Chocolate Raspberry Linzer Cookies, 9
Chocolate Raspberry Meringue, 92
Chocolate Sauce, 82
Chocolate Sour Cream Frosting, 54
Chocolate Swirl Bavarians, 93
Chocolate Triple Layer Cake, 37
Choco-Nut Crust, 32
Classic Mud Pie, 31
Coffeecakes
Apricot Orange Bread, 61
Chocolate and Cherry Braid, 63
Chocolate Apple Bread, 56
Chocolate Banana Bread, 66
Chocolate Bubble Biscuits, 64
Chocolate Chip Brioche, 57
Chocolate Filled Kuchen, 68
Chocolate Pistachio Bread, 69
Chocolate Raisin Bread, 69
Cranberry Nut Holiday Bread, 64
Granola Coffee Ring, 58
Little Bits™ Irish Soda Bread, 66
Toll House™ Crumbcake, 63
Cookies
Anise Cookie Cordials, 23
Black & White Cheesecake Brownies, 11

Butterscotch Apricot Streusel Bars, 5
Butterscotch Date Surprise, 6
Butterscotch Granola Cookies, 13
Butterscotch Lemon Cookies, 14
Cappuccino Brownies, 20
Cheese Crunchers, 8
Chocolate Almond Macaroons, 27
Chocolate Cinnabar Wreaths, 16
Chocolate Date Envelopes, 27
Chocolate-Dipped Brandy Snaps, 17
Chocolate-Dipped Sandwich Macaroons, 20
Chocolate Macaroon Squares, 20
Chocolate Mint Cookies, 22
Chocolate Mint Meltaways, 23
Chocolate Mint Pinwheels, 11
Chocolate Mint Sugar Cookie Drops, 25
Chocolate Orange Granola Cookies, 19
Chocolate Raspberry Coconut Squares, 12
Chocolate Raspberry Linzer Cookies, 9
Double Chocolate Cookies, 19
Double Chocolate Mint Chip Cookies, 25
Irish Coffee Brownies, 25
Little Bits™ Meringue Wreaths, 23
Magic Cookie Bars, 12
Maple Walnut Bars, 12
Milk Chocolate Florentine Cookies, 26
Milk Chocolate Pecan Bars, 5
Minty Fudge Brownies, 11
Mocha Shortbread Cookies, 25
Mocha Walnut Cookies, 14
No-Bake Butterscotch Snack Bars, 16
No-Bake Fudge Brownies, 19
Oatmeal Extravaganzas, 27
Oatmeal Scotchies™, 14
Original Toll House® Cookies, 6
Spice Islands Butterscotch Bars, 19
Cranberry Nut Holiday Bread, 64
Cream Cheese Frosting, 38
Cream Chip Frosting, 51
Cream Sherry Fruit Cake, 40
Creamy Chocolate Fudge, 71
Creamy Milk Chocolate Hazelnut Frosting, 54
Crepes
Butterscotch Orange Crepes, 85
Crusts, 33, 78, 86, 89, 90
Angel Pie Crust, 36
Chocolate Cookie Crust, 31
Choco-Nut Crust, 32
Graham Cracker Crust, 33
Cupcakes
Cheesecake Cupcakes, 38

D
Desserts
Brandy Alexander Gems, 91

Butterscotch Orange Crepes, 85
Chocolate Almond Frozen Mousse, 78
Chocolate Bavarian Cream, 88
Chocolate Cherry Cheesecake, 89
Chocolate Filled Cream Puff Ring, 80
Chocolate Fruit Pastry, 86
Chocolate Meringue Cups with Chocolate Sauce, 82
Chocolate Mint Baked Alaska, 86
Chocolate Mint Baked Custard, 82
Chocolate Mint Ice Cream, 91
Chocolate Pistachio Cannolis, 92
Chocolate Raspberry Meringue, 92
Chocolate Swirl Bavarians, 93
Frozen Chocolate Mousse Cake, 79
Frozen Chocolate Soufflé Cordial, 83
Fudgy Rice Pudding Supreme, 80
Heavenly Chocolate Cheesecake, 90
Icy Good Chocolate Cups, 88
Little Bits™ Baked Pancake with Fruit, 83
Milk Chocolate Cream Pastries, 87
Miniature Chocolate Soufflés, 93
Mocha Chocolate Chip Cheesecake, 78
Strawberry Chocolate Shortcake, 51
Toll House™ Quick Ice Cream, 91
Doughnuts
Chocolate Orange Glazed Doughnuts, 69
Double Chocolate Cookies, 19
Double Chocolate Mint Chip Cookies, 25
Dublin Special Frosting, 54

E
Easy Chocolate Sweet Rolls, 56

F
Frosted Chocolate Pumpkin Cake, 38
Frostings, 45
Butterscotch Cream Cheese Frosting, 54
Butterscotch Orange Frosting, 55
Chocolate Brandy Creme, 55
Chocolate Buttercream Frosting, 55
Chocolate Mint Frosting, 55
Chocolate Sour Cream Frosting, 54
Cream Cheese Frosting, 38
Cream Chip Frosting, 51
Creamy Milk Chocolate Hazelnut Frosting, 54
Dublin Special Frosting, 54
Milk Chocolate Frosting, 55
Mocha Frosting, 37
Whipped Chocolate Cream Frosting, 55
Frozen Chocolate Mousse Cake, 79

Frozen Chocolate Soufflé Cordial, 83
Frozen Mocha Mousse Pie, 35
Frozen Strawberry Fudge Pie, 34
Fruit Cakes
Butterscotch Fruit Spice Cake, 53
Cream Sherry Fruit Cake, 40
Fudge
Butterscotch Fudge, 77
Chocolate Fudge Marzipan
Squares, 74
Creamy Chocolate Fudge, 71
Macadamia Orange Fudge, 77
Minty Mallows, 74
Nutty Chocolate Mint Fudge, 74
Ultimate Rocky Road, 71
Fudge Sauce, 31
Fudgy Rice Pudding Supreme, 80

G
Glazes, 22, 23, 42, 45, 58, 69, 80
Chocolate Glaze, 53
Graham Cracker Crust, 33
Granola Coffee Ring, 58

H
Heavenly Chocolate Cheesecake, 90

I
Ice Cream
Chocolate Mint Baked Alaska, 86
Chocolate Mint Ice Cream, 91
Toll House™ Quick Ice Cream, 91
Icy Good Chocolate Cups, 88
Irish Coffee Brownies, 25

L
Lemon Cups Deluxe, 73
Little Bits™ Baked Pancake with
Fruit, 83
Little Bits™ Irish Soda Bread, 66
Little Bits™ Meringue Wreaths, 23

M
Macadamia Orange Fudge, 77
Macaroons
Chocolate Almond Macaroons, 27
Chocolate-Dipped Sandwich
Macaroons, 20
Magic Cookie Bars, 12
Maple Walnut Bars, 12
Midnight Torte, 53
Milk Chocolate Chiffon Cake, 47
Milk Chocolate Cream Pastries, 87
Milk Chocolate Florentine Cookies,
26
Milk Chocolate Frosting, 55
Milk Chocolate Mallow Fudge
Sauce, 85
Milk Chocolate Pecan Bars, 5
Miniature Chocolate Soufflés, 93
Minty Fudge Brownies, 11
Minty Mallows, 74
Minty Mousse Pie au Chocolat, 28
Mocha Almond Torte, 37
Mocha Cheese Pie, 34
Mocha Chocolate Chip Cheesecake,
78

Mocha Frosting, 37
Mocha Loaf Cakes, 54
Mocha Shortbread Cookies, 25
Mocha Truffles, 73
Mocha Walnut Cookies, 14
Mocha Walnut Sauce, 85
Mousses
Chocolate Almond Frozen
Mousse, 78
Frozen Chocolate Mousse Cake, 79
Frozen Chocolate Soufflé Cordial,
83
Muffins
Chocolate Macadamia Muffins, 61
Chocolate Pumpkin Muffins, 67
Orange Chip Muffins, 66

N
No-Bake Butterscotch Snack Bars, 16
No-Bake Fudge Brownies, 19
Nutty Chocolate Mint Fudge, 74
Nutty Chocolate Sour Cream Pie, 28

O
Oatmeal Butterscotch Tea Biscuits, 64
Oatmeal Extravaganzas, 27
Oatmeal Scotchies™, 14
Old-Fashioned Almond Crunch, 70
Orange Chip Muffins, 66
Orange Sauce, 85
Original Toll House® Cookies, 6

P
Pastries
Brandy Alexander Gems, 91
Chocolate Filled Cream Puff Ring,
80
Chocolate Fruit Pastry, 86
Chocolate Pistachio Cannolis, 92
Milk Chocolate Cream Pastries, 87
Pies
Best-of-All Black Bottom Pie, 33
Butterscotch Crumb Apple Pie, 30
Butterscotch Rum Chiffon Pie, 34
Cafe Cream Pie, 32
Chocolate Chip Tarts à l'Orange,
28
Chocolate Cream Strawberry Tart,
29
Chocolate Macadamia Angel Pie,
36
Chocolate Oatmeal Cookie Pie, 35
Classic Mud Pie, 31
Frozen Mocha Mousse Pie, 35
Frozen Strawberry Fudge Pie, 34
Minty Mousse Pie au Chocolat, 28
Mocha Cheese Pie, 34
Nutty Chocolate Sour Cream Pie,
28
Quick Butterscotch Ice Cream Pie,
33
Toll House™ Pie, 31
Pound Cakes
Chocolate Almond Marble Pound
Cake, 40
Toll House™ Pound Cake, 46
Prestige Pecan Drops, 71

Pudding
Chocolate Mint Baked Custard, 82
Fudgy Rice Pudding Supreme, 80
Pumpernickel Bread, 60

Q
Quick Butterscotch Ice Cream Pie, 33

S
Satiny Fudge Sauce, 92
Sauces
Butterscotch Cinnamon Glaze, 82
Butterscotch Nut Sauce, 80
Chocolate Almond Glaze, 82
Chocolate Caramel Sauce, 92
Chocolate Custard Sauce Grand
Marnier, 87
Chocolate Fondue Fantasia, 93
Chocolate Sauce, 82
Fudge Sauce, 31
Milk Chocolate Mallow Fudge
Sauce, 85
Mocha Walnut Sauce, 85
Orange Sauce, 85
Satiny Fudge Sauce, 92
Shortcake
Strawberry Chocolate Shortcake,
51
Snacks
Butterscotch Popcorn Crunchies,
76
Chocolate-Dipped Fruit, 75
No-Bake Butterscotch Snack Bars,
16
Soufflés
Frozen Chocolate Soufflé Cordial,
83
Miniature Chocolate Soufflés, 93
Spice Islands Butterscotch Bars, 19
Strawberry Chocolate Shortcake, 51

T
Tarts
Chocolate Chip Tarts à l'Orange,
28
Chocolate Cream Strawberry Tart,
29
Toll House™ Cake, 45
Toll House™ Carrot Cake, 48
Toll House™ Crumbcake, 63
Toll House™ Pie, 31
Toll House™ Pound Cake, 46
Toll House™ Quick Ice Cream, 91
Toppings: *see* **Frostings, Sauces**
Tortes
Brownie Cream Chip Torte, 51
Chocolate Baum Torte, 48
Midnight Torte, 53
Mocha Almond Torte, 37
Toll House™ Cake, 45

U
Ultimate Rocky Road, 71

W
Whipped Chocolate Cream Frosting,
55